PICASSO

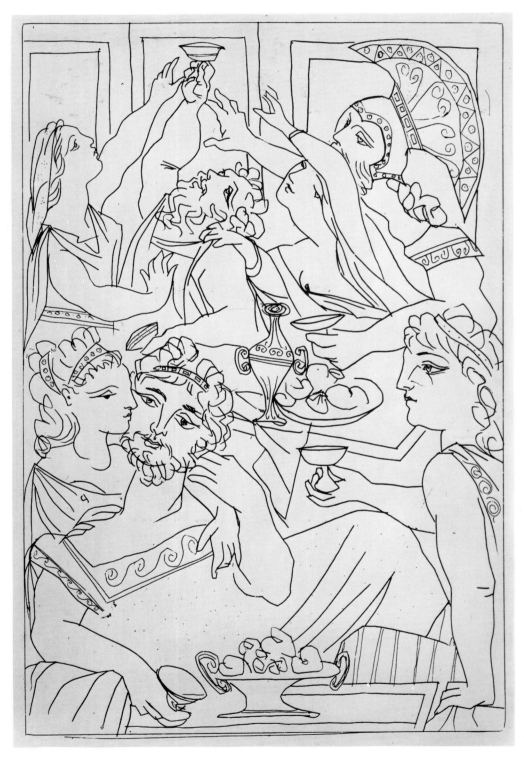

CELEBRATION OF PEACE. 1934. Etching, 8³/₄ × 5¹/₂″.
Illustration for Aristophanes, *Lysistrata*.
The Heritage Club, Norwalk, Connecticut

PABLO

PICASSO

HANS L. C. JAFFÉ

Professor of Modern Art, University of Amsterdam

HARRY N. ABRAMS, INC., PUBLISHERS, NEW YORK

Library of Congress Cataloging in Publication Data
Jaffé, Hans Ludwig C.
   Pablo Picasso.
   Concise ed. of the author's Pablo Picasso originally
published: New York : Abrams, 1964.
   1. Picasso, Pablo, 1881-1973. I. Picasso, Pablo,
1881-1973.   II. Title.
ND553.P5J253 1983   759.4   82-21029
ISBN 0-8109-5333-1 (EP)
ISBN 0-8109-1480-8 (HNA)

Published in 1983 by Harry N. Abrams, Inc., Publishers, New York.
Also published in a leatherbound edition for The Easton Press,
Norwalk, Connecticut. All rights reserved. No part of the
contents of this book may be reproduced without the written
permission of the publisher.
Picture reproduction rights reserved by S.P.A.D.E.M., Paris

Printed and bound in Japan

CONTENTS

———————————

COLORPLATES

PICASSO

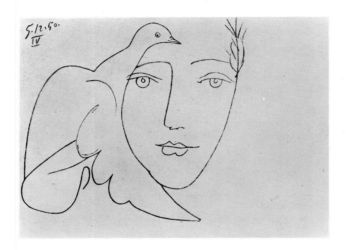

I. FACE OF PEACE. 1950. Drawing, pencil on paper.
Photo courtesy Cercle d'Art, Paris

Picasso

FOR MANY YEARS the art and person of Picasso have been an essential aspect of our twentieth-century world. Though his work has been steadily transforming itself since the beginning of this century, it has become a fixed point against which we measure other art. And Picasso himself became one of the dominant figures of our age. How did the multiform, varied work of this capricious and stubborn man come to be taken as so reliable, so lucid a criterion?

That is the fascinating and disturbing question raised by this great man and his work. Throughout the more than seventy years of his creative activity—that is, throughout the period of the rise of modern art—Picasso was at the center of the artistic and spiritual life of our time. He became the prism, the lens of this life, capturing and focusing all its light, and reflecting it, transformed, into the darkest corners of our world.

And yet this universal and central figure always kept for himself a great solitude, the solitude of his native Spain: "Nothing can be accomplished without solitude; I have made a kind of solitude for myself." He guarded this solitude even in relation to his own works, for once he created them, he dissociated himself from them; and they began to lead a life independent of their creator. In the art of Picasso, the personal became impersonal, his own experience became the experience of his age, of mankind.

This solitude was at the root of Picasso's independence; it also accounts for the fact that in his painting, sculpture, print-making, and ceram-

ic work he followed no rules, was bound by n[o] routine. For him art was always an adventure "To find is the thing."

The man who said: "I do not see why so muc[h] importance should be attached to the idea o[f] 'research' in painting" must have been sure o[f] his own ability to find and to make use of wha[t] he found. It is only thus that Picasso achieve[d] absolute freedom in relation to the objects a[-] round him, as well as in relation to his ow[n] painting: "I treat paintings as I treat object[s] If a window in a picture looks wrong, I close [it] and draw the curtains, just as I would do in m[y] own room."

As a result of this freedom, this independenc[e] Picasso remained completely flexible. That [is] why there was no "evolution" in his painting, n[o] historically determined sequence, only continu[a] and spontaneous transformation, a perpetu[al] renewal: "For me, art has neither past nor futur[e] All I have ever made was made for the present. And this present, this throbbing life which su[r]rounded the artist's solitude, was incarnated i[n] his work, thanks to the curiosity, the avidity wit[h] which he pursued it, devoured it. Not only th[e] life of art, but life itself is captured by this len[s] this prism which seems to draw light to it.

The man who became his epoch's guide recog[-] nized no preconceived paths: "A painting is no[t] the result of working toward a goal, it is a strok[e] of luck, an experience." His works are not lik[e] milestones placed at regular intervals along [a] road; rather, they are like the pebbles tossed ou[t] at random by a grown-up Tom Thumb to mak[e]

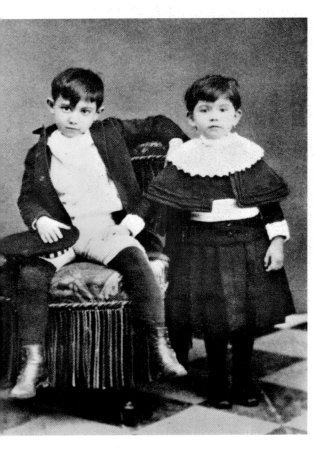

2. Picasso and his sister, 1888

different kind, Goethe wrote these lines, which Picasso could have made his own:

Ich ging im Walde so für mich hin,
und nichts zu suchen, das war mein Sinn . . .
(I went to the woods just to walk,
nor was my purpose to find a treasure . . .)

Picasso himself said: "The work one does is another way of keeping a diary." Facts and events, even those encountered at random, are thus incorporated in the work, and constitute finds which lead to the discovery of the truth.

For truth is the goal—and the source—of this art; and thus Picasso has taken his place in that succession of great artists who have given truth precedence over pictorial beauty. Of the latter, he took a rather disparaging view: "The academic gospel of beauty is a fraud." Our notion of beauty changes, he realized, being merely an instrument, one aspect of a given conception of the world. What we call beauty is always threatening to turn into conformity—and Picasso, as a

possible for his friends to trace his steps, to follow him through the trackless waste. The path that Picasso traced since 1900 cuts across our entire epoch: "I have never painted anything but my time."

It is perhaps this fact that best defines Picasso's creative genius: not only did he observe his own time, bear witness to it; he lived it, and lived it most intensely, with all its vicissitudes, its hopes and disappointments. And he always grasped its truth, its authenticity: "Art is a lie that makes us realize truth." These words bring to mind the lines that Vincent van Gogh wrote to his brother: "All right, call them lies if you will, but they are more exact than literal truth." Picasso, who explicitly rejected the idea of groping for a visual truth, nonetheless sought the essential truth of our conception of the world and of our life; like Vincent, he sought it passionately. And this is why he found . . .

He found in the manner of a genius—that is, unexpectedly. Concerning a find of an entirely

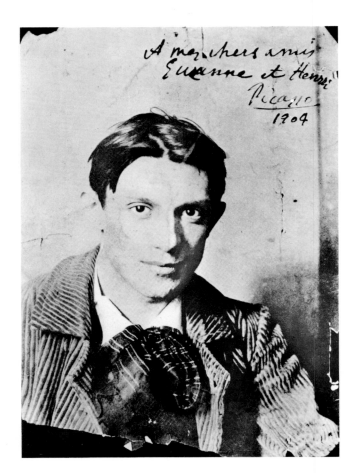

3. Picasso, 1904

Spaniard with a solid anarchist upbringing, abhorred all conformity. Truth is revealed only through disconcerting discoveries.

Authentic truth was Picasso's domain, and this domain is limitless. When he said, speaking of painting in general but actually referring to his own painting, "A painter paints to rid himself of his sensations and his visions," he stressed the visionary, prophetic aspect of his discoveries. In his art he was always fully committed: like Jacob wrestling with the angel, he did not let go of what he had in his grasp until he had conquered it. The intense and diverse life that characterized his works over more than a half-century stemmed from this commitment: "I want the work to reflect only feeling." These words locate the source of his authenticity and at the same time explain why Picasso never devoted himself to any one genre. His curiosity, his sensibility were so universal that they could not be confined to a single area of painting, nor even to painting alone. Picasso was one of the few universal artists of our time—and it was his authenticity that made him universal.

This is also why Picasso was never a partisan of so-called abstract art: "From the point of view of art, forms are neither abstract nor concrete; they are simply forms—lies—some of which are more convincing than others." And elsewhere he wrote: "There is no abstract art. One must always begin with something. Then all traces of reality can be removed. There isn't any danger then, because the idea of the object has left an indelible mark. It is what moved the artist originally, inspired his ideas, set his emotions to vibrating. In the end his ideas and emotions become imprisoned in his painting. No matter what happens, they can no longer escape from the picture."

These lines are proof of Picasso's commitment, his attachment to the objects of his paintings— the objects of life. This great art is fully rooted in man's life, in our time. It is also an eloquent refutation of the romantic myth that sees artists of genius as ahead of, outside of, their time: in actual fact, they are the first to see that time clearly, they are among the few who do not lag behind. . . . Picasso illustrated this truth not only in *Guernica*, which is its sublime proof, but in his work as a whole.

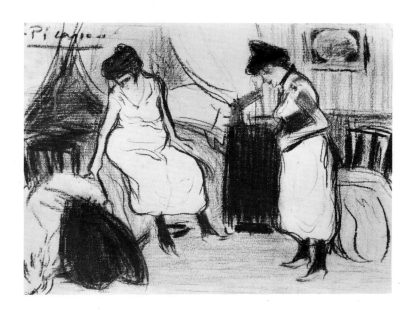

4. TWO WOMEN. 1900. Colored crayon on white paper, 10⅝ × 8⅛″. *The Abrams Family Collection, New York*

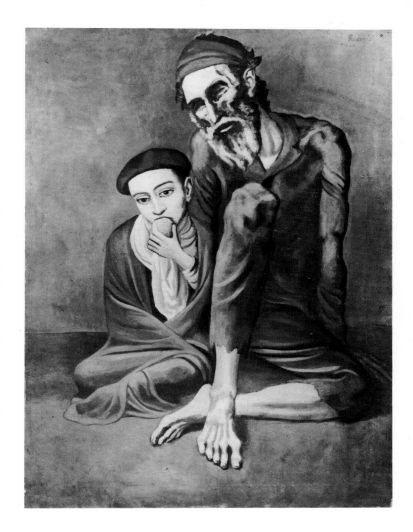

5. OLD JEW. 1903. Oil on canvas, 49¼ × 36¼″.
The Hermitage, Leningrad

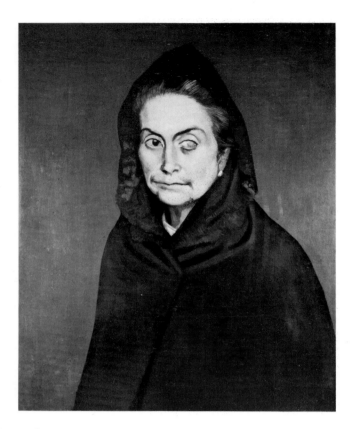

6. CELESTINA. 1903. Oil on canvas, $31^7/_8 \times 23^5/_8''$.
Private collection

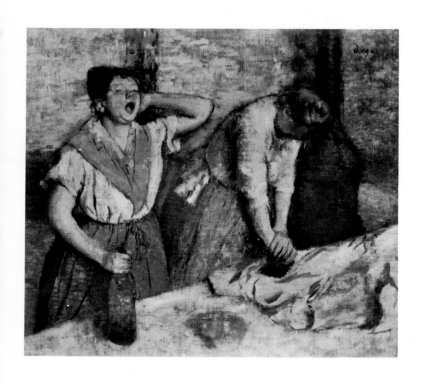

7. Edgar Degas: TWO LAUNDRESSES. C. 1884.
Oil on canvas, $29^7/_8 \times 32^1/_4''$. *The Louvre, Paris*

Guernica (figure 34) is a striking and deeply moving testimony to Picasso's involvement in the fate of our epoch; at the same time it shows how deep were his roots in Spain, his native land. To anyone who traces the path Picasso followed since the beginning of this century—as the reader will do in examining the reproductions in this book—it will be clear that nearly every new phase in the master's art seems to have been nourished by a visit to Spain, a return to his source. This continual renewal, these fresh starts, suggest the ancient myth of Antaeus, whose strength is restored when he comes into contact with the earth, his mother: Picasso's gigantic work was re-created each time he reestablished contact with Spain. And the monumental *Guernica,* which may be regarded as the high point of his art, came into being at a moment when his native land was in mortal danger . . .

But the bombing of Guernica—the actual event which occurred on April 28, 1937—was more than a threat to Spain. The raid by Nazi planes in the service of Franco on the open and defenseless Basque city was the initial act of aggression committed against humanity by barbarians. Picasso never trusted abstractions: for him human beings were the essential reality. That is why he painted *Guernica,* and that too is why he declared after the end of the Second World War: "No, painting is not interior decoration. It is an instrument of war, for attack and for defense against the enemy."

Picasso's art, his work as a whole, was not easily accessible to his contemporaries—and this is true of any authentic and original work. Nonetheless it deals with reality, with the life of men, and it is always relevant to it. Among the great creators of modern art, Picasso was not only the most universal, but also the most ardently human. It was because he lived our epoch intensely that he became its light, its beacon. This light, which he gathered with such fervor from every contemporary source, was radiated, transformed by his enthusiasm, by his freedom, by his untiring creative genius: "In our mutilated epoch, nothing is more important than to create enthusiasm." This is what Picasso did for more than seventy years.

Pablo Ruiz Picasso was born at Málaga in southern Spain on October 25, 1881. His father,

José Ruiz Blasco, taught drawing and painting at the provincial school of arts and crafts, which was the center of art education in that part of Andalusia. His mother, Maria Picasso Lopez, whose name he later chose to bear, kept the house, situated at No. 36 (now No. 15), Plaza de la Merced. There the young Pablo grew up in the early part of his youth—in that very southern city, with a climate like Africa's, and an eventful history going back to Mediterranean antiquity (figure 2).

In 1891—Pablo was a little less than ten—the family left Málaga and southern Spain: his father became an instructor at the Da Guarda school of arts and crafts at La Coruña, in Galicia. Pablo lived in this Atlantic port, which to a native of southern Spain must have seemed typically northern, until he was fifteen. What a change in his surroundings—for a boy with wide-open eyes— from the Mediterranean Andalusia to the rough, rocky coast of the Iberian Atlantic! And we have proof that the young Pablo did use his eyes in his drawings of that time, some of which have survived. The story is that José Ruiz, struck by his son's extraordinary gifts, gave him his own paints and brushes, thus conferring on him the vocation of painter. Don José Ruiz, though a talented painter, was provincial in his outlook: he specialized in pictures of pigeons and still lifes with flowers. After his son's "initiation," Don Ruiz appears to have given up painting, devoting himself exclusively to teaching.

In 1895 Don José Ruiz was made instructor of drawing and painting at the La Lonja art school in Barcelona. After spending the summer in Málaga, Pablo's birthplace, the family moved to Barcelona, the financial and intellectual capital of Catalonia. Thus the young Pablo left the confined atmosphere of provincial Spain for a metropolis artistically and intellectually linked with Europe's cultural centers, not only because of its bustling port, but because the independent Catalans had always regarded themselves as a people more international in spirit than the Spanish, as a people whose traditional ambitions were not bounded by the Pyrenees.

In 1896 the fifteen-year-old Pablo was admitted to the art school where his father taught. He demonstrated his exceptional gifts as a painter by his brilliant performance in the entrance

examinations. As elsewhere in Europe, these required of the candidate meticulous observation of the subject in all its detail, and a naturalistic technique which not many boys of that age possessed.

In 1897 he went even further: with the backing of his family, who were full of admiration for his gifts and thought him deserving of the best teachers in Spain, the young artist applied for admission to the Royal Academy of San Fernan-

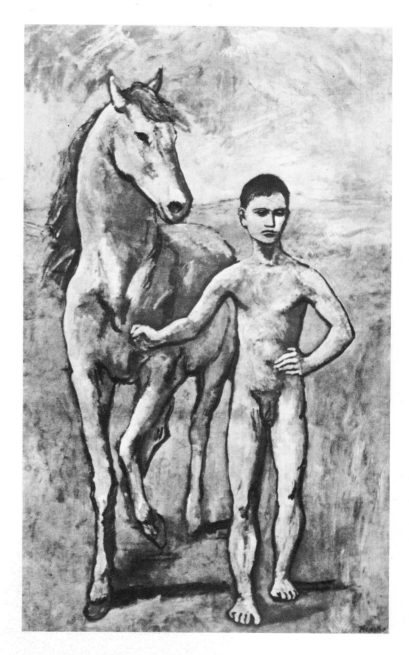

8. BOY LEADING A HORSE. 1905. Oil on canvas, 76³/₄ × 38¹/₄″. *The Museum of Modern Art, New York (Gift of William S. Paley, the donor retaining life interest)*

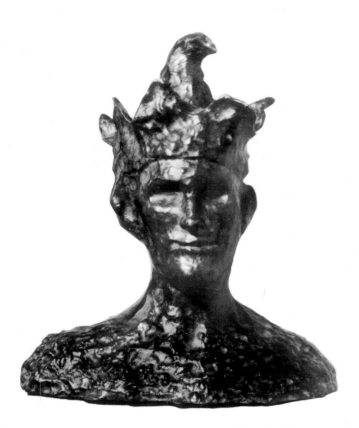

9. HARLEQUIN. 1905. Bronze, height 16¹/₈″.
Collection Mrs. Bertram Smith, New York

Els Quatre Gats. At this establishment frequented by the Catalan bohemians he had his first one-man show in 1897—a series of portraits of friends and acquaintances belonging to this noisy and active circle. This exhibition brought him his first notice, in the magazine *La Vanguardia*. It was at Els Quatre Gats that the young Picasso met the Catalan painters and writers who influenced him at the outset of his career: Eugenio d'Ors, a critic and essayist; Miguel Utrillo, an art historian; Jaime Sabartés, a young poet who remained his faithful friend through the years; Carlos Casagemas, and the brothers González, painters who introduced him to the young Catalan school; and others.

The artists of the Catalan school, in contrast with the traditional artists of Madrid, found their inspiration in the North, in the English "decadent" style. They were influenced, too, by

do in Madrid, the most important art school in Spain at the end of the nineteenth century. The teaching there was academic and traditionalist. Picasso passed the admissions requirements of this academy with as much ease and brilliance as he had those of the Barcelona school; the entrance examination so dreaded by his fellow candidates posed no difficulties for him. Moreover, he had already shown a painting, *Science and Charity*—a work treating a symbolic subject—at an exhibition in Madrid in the spring of 1897, that is, prior to his admission to the Academy in October, and had been awarded Honorable Mention. The next year a painting of his won medals at exhibitions in Madrid and in Málaga. Thus the young painter had every chance of professional success in Madrid. But he took an intense dislike to the city, and having been ill with scarlet fever, went back to Barcelona. Early in 1898 he went to Horta de Ebro (also called Horta de San Juan) in the foothills of the Pyrenees, to convalesce.

When he returned from the country to Barcelona he joined a circle of young artists and intellectuals whose meeting place was the café

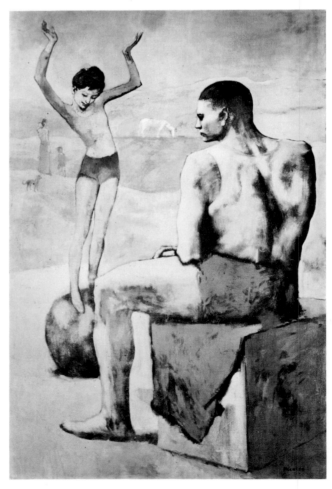

10. CIRCUS ACROBATS. 1905. Oil on canvas, 57¹/₂ × 38¹/₈″.
Pushkin Museum, Moscow

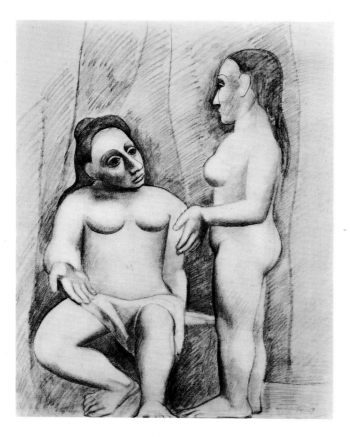

11. WOMAN SEATED AND WOMAN STANDING. 1906. Drawing, charcoal on paper, 23³/₄ × 18¹/₈″. *Philadelphia Museum of Art (Louise and Walter Arensberg Collection)*

Parisian success came when he sold three sketches to Berthe Weill, an enterprising art dealer. Pedro Mañach, a Spaniard, offered him a 150-franc "contract" in exchange for his production. Little is known about the work he did during his Paris visit; *Le Moulin de la Galette,* a painting in the manner of Lautrec, may date from this first trip.

Around Christmas Picasso went back to Barcelona. The following year he went to Málaga, and then to Madrid where he met Pío Baroja and Rubén Darío, members of the group of '98, and Francisco Soler. With Soler he founded the avant-garde magazine *Arte Joven.* The first of the two issues published, dated March 31, 1901, was illustrated by the young artist. This magazine, which did not confine itself to purely artistic questions, reveals the spirit of the youthful Picasso and his friends; it was polemical, revolutionary, anti-bourgeois, satirical, and independent; its chief ambition was to carry the modern spirit of Barcelona to the Spanish capital. The

the art of Steinlen, and had progressive social ideals. Their drawings and illustrations appeared frequently in newspapers and magazines. The style of these works—especially the sinuous, flexible line—clearly relates them to the Symbolist school and to Art Nouveau. Toulouse-Lautrec was their model.

Picasso's first drawings published in 1900 in the Spanish magazine *Joventut* (a younger sister of the Munich *Jugend*) are also in this style, inspired by Parisian painting and lithography. They place Picasso as an illustrator among that little group of penetrating and pessimistic observers whose awakened and critical minds display, in their rapid sketches from life, an occasional flash of sardonic humor. Though Picasso and some of his friends practiced this style in Catalonia, its center was Paris.

To Paris Picasso went, with his friend Casagemas. He arrived there toward the end of October and stayed in the studio of the Spanish painter Isidre Nonnell at 49, Rue Gabrielle. His first

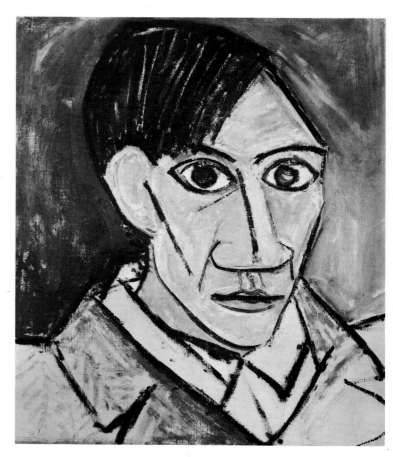

12. SELF-PORTRAIT. 1907. Oil on canvas, 19³/₄ × 18¹/₈″. *National Gallery, Prague*

attempt was bound to fail. For one thing, Picasso left for Paris on almost the day the first issue appeared. But the very fact that the two friends published the magazine, as well as their intention to write a book entitled *Madrid*, is eloquent proof of the young Picasso's independent attitude, his social ideals, and his revolutionary spirit tinged with Catalan anarchism.

His second trip to Paris brought him an exhibition at Ambroise Vollard's which was reviewed most favorably in *La Revue Blanche*. At about the same time an equally flattering review of his exhibition of pastels at the Salon Parés in Barcelona was published in *Pel y Ploma,* edited by Ramón Casas. These early paintings and pastels, some of which have survived, display the young painter's talent and versatility; they do not as yet disclose his originality. The·twenty-year-old artist had by then been exposed to, and assimi-

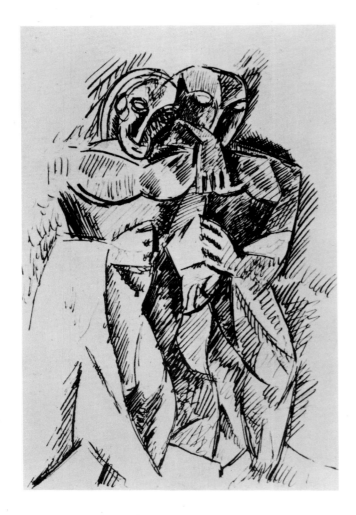

13. TWO FEMALE NUDES. 1908. Drawing, ink on paper, 19 × 12⁷/₈″. *Musée Picasso, Paris*

lated, several influences: that of Toulouse-Lautrec, from whom he derived chiefly the ambiance of his subject—the cafés, the Parisian cabarets; that of the Impressionists, which is manifested in his brilliant gamut of colors; that of Art Nouveau, as shown by his tendency to use a stylized line. But the spirit that dominates all these works is still that of the little group of the café Els Quatre Gats in Barcelona, inspired by the ambition to emulate the freedom and independence of the Paris school of the time. Until the end of 1901 Picasso was a disciple—talented but provincial—of this school.

However, at the end of that year, when Picasso returned to Barcelona, a deep and significant change took place in his painting. This change strikes us first of all in his choice of colors: the variable range of brilliant tones yields to a single dark and oppressive blue. But this transformation in his painting—the first in a long series—was more than a mere change in color, more than the adoption of a new tonality. It was above all the result of a new attitude toward people. Instead of observing them ruthlessly and satirically, he now treated his models with sympathy, with melancholic tenderness. His subjects changed, too. Instead of painting café scenes, Parisian interiors with women in big hats seated at tables and drinking, he began to represent, to imagine enigmatic, emaciated figures standing rigid and silent against a vague or empty background. These men and women no longer evoke contemporary life, they have nothing in common with the tense, nervous atmosphere of Paris at the beginning of this century; they are beggars, blind men, and poor street artists, transformed by the painter's compassionate and affectionate vision into almost mythical figures that belong to no particular, or familiar, epoch. The atmosphere in which Picasso places them is more or less that in which similar figures appear in Rilke's poems, written the same year, 1901—an atmosphere of solitude, hunger, and everyday misery, borne with dogged courage. And this spiritual atmosphere is suggested not only by the angular lines of the emaciated bodies, but above all by the sad, distressing color, the subdued blue, which dominates the pictorial space and the figures by its remote and silent unreality.

Child with a Dove, probably painted near the

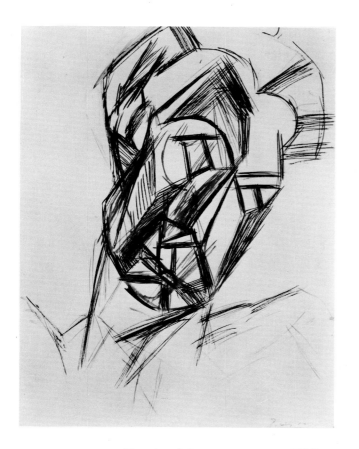

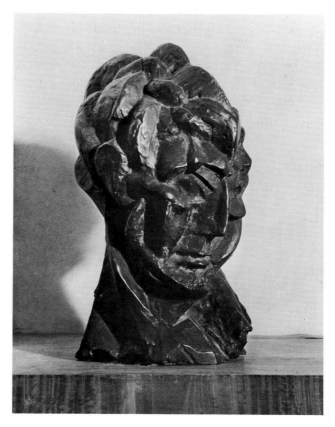

14. HEAD. 1909. Drawing, ink on paper, 25 × 18½″.
Private collection, Paris

15. WOMAN'S HEAD. 1909. Bronze, height 16¼″.
The Museum of Modern Art, New York

end of 1901, is the first of the series of canvases that comprise Picasso's Blue Period (page 49). Here, the artist's tenderness manifests itself for the first time, in clear contrast with the spirit of sharp and satirical observation that characterized the street and café scenes. Was it the theme of childhood that led Picasso to discover this poetry of tenderness? Or was it the detail of the dove that awakened memories of his childhood, when he often watched his father painting pigeons? However that may be, Picasso was conscious of his change in style: from 1901 he signed simply "Picasso," where previously he had used also his patronymic of Ruiz (or its abbreviation).

His second trip to Paris, in 1901, also brought a change in his personal landscape, as his circle of young Catalan bohemian friends was replaced with a group of Parisian poets and eccentrics, among them Max Jacob, whom he had met at Vollard's, and Gustave Coquiot, the art critic of whom he painted two portraits during this visit. The work of his Blue Period—during which he produced a number of paintings showing

solitary figures such as the portrait of his friend Sabartés, or the guitarist, or the old Jew (figure 5)—was done partly in Paris and partly in Barcelona. In 1902 Berthe Weill and Vollard again exhibited his paintings. He was then in Barcelona, and did not return to Paris until the end of the year. He stayed a few months; early in 1903 he was back in Barcelona, to remain until early in 1904.

The fact that most of the works of the Blue Period were painted in Barcelona accounts for the resemblance of many of his models to figures by El Greco. His affinity with this master of Spanish Mannerism is apparent in the great composition of 1901, which dates from the beginning of the Blue Period—the evocation or burial of the painter Casagemas, now in the Petit Palais in Paris. Like El Greco's *Burial of Count Orgaz*, this painting is divided into two zones, one earthly and the other transcendent; the element of pathos that appears here for the first time arises from Picasso's deeply felt attachment to his friend. In the paintings of the immediately following years this affinity with El Greco asserts itself more and more. The elongated proportions, the ecstatic and angular gestures, the relation between space and figures, all this brings to mind the great Spanish master, but the feeling in Picasso's works remains authentically his own. He makes use of El Greco's elongated forms and hallucinatory space, but he employs these elements to express a feeling peculiar to his time—solidarity with distressed, famished, oppressed humanity. *Célestina* (figure 6) is a superb example of this feeling and of the style in which it found its form: this portrait of an old one-eyed woman, dressed in somber color, achieves, thanks to the simplicity of its color and the economy of its line, an austere nobility which relates it to El Greco's most restrained portraits. From the same year, 1903, dates the enigmatic,

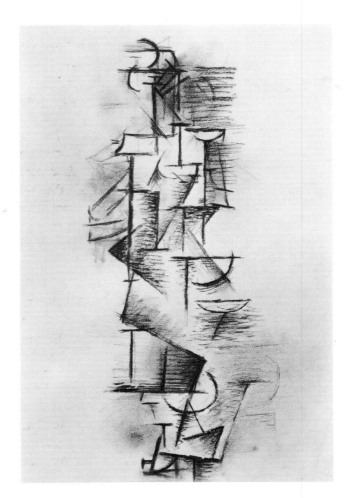

17. FEMALE NUDE. 1910. Drawing, charcoal on paper, 19 × 12¹/₈″. *The Metropolitan Museum of Art, New York (The Alfred Stieglitz Collection)*

symbolic composition entitled *La Vie* (page 51), showing a nude couple and a woman with a child in her arms; this painting, with its long, slender figures, has the same feeling of melancholy tenderness. But *Célestina,* above all, and the canvas representing a blind guitarist (The Art Institute of Chicago), show Picasso's affinity with El Greco and the way he makes use of it to express his solidarity with, his active compassion for, the poor, to whom he belonged himself in that period of his life. At the beginning of the century he, like Rilke, was one of the young artists who felt distressed at the sight of human misery, and expressed this feeling in sober, ascetic, austere works, with a restraint that precluded sentimentality or bathos.

This somber and austere period terminated at the end of 1904, after Picasso had settled permanently in Paris (figure 3). He arrived there

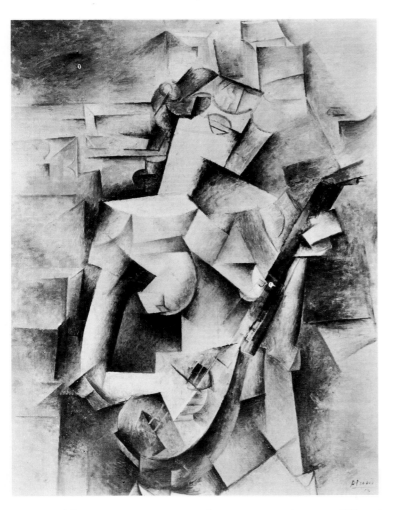

16. GIRL WITH MANDOLIN (FANNY TELLIER). 1910. Oil on canvas, 39¹/₂ × 29″. *The Museum of Modern Art, New York (Nelson A. Rockefeller Bequest)*

in April—this was his fourth trip—and moved into the so-called Bateau-lavoir, the dilapidated building at 13, Rue Ravignan (now Place Emile-Goudeau), which was one of the centers of artistic bohemia at the time. Two works are characteristic of the Blue Period at its close—*Woman Ironing* (page 53), an oil, and *Frugal Repast,* an etching from 1904. A comparison of the first with Degas' painting entitled *Two Laundresses* at once reveals the authenticity of Picasso's austere imagination: Degas observes laundresses at work, wearied by their routine (figure 7); Picasso's laundress is a visionary apparition, bowed under the burden of work, and rendered with the sadness of another oppressed being who sympathizes with her. The *Frugal Repast* expresses the same ascetic melancholy, not only in its subject, but also in the spareness of its lines and accents, and in its sober and restrained contrasts between black and white. His Blue Period, which extended from 1901 to the end of 1904, shows Picasso in full possession of an artistic individuality based not upon talent—he had proved his talent long before this—but upon an attitude toward human beings, upon an authentic conception of the world.

The following years marked a happy turn in Picasso's life and painting. He made friends. He met Guillaume Apollinaire, who became one of his most loyal companions. He even began to sell his paintings: to two Americans—Gertrude Stein, a daringly independent writer, and her brother Leo, a well-informed art lover—and to a Russian, the wholesale lumber dealer and collector Shchukin. In 1905 he met Fernande Olivier at the well of the Bateau-lavoir; she lived with him until 1911. That summer he went to Holland, to Schoorldam, at the invitation of his friend Schilperoort. The greater brightness of his life was reflected in his work: austere, ascetic melancholy is tempered by a pure and intimate tenderness. Just as with the onset of the Blue Period, the change manifested itself primarily in his palette: the subdued cold blue gave way to brown, red ocher, and rose.

With the new palette came a transformation in subject. The famished, solitary figures shown against a neutral and mythologically vague background were succeeded by comedians, circus and carnival performers, shown in intimate family scenes, calm and relaxed, in an idyllic atmosphere. Once again the artistic metamorphosis reflected a change in the artist's human attitude: his despair, the pessimism of his years of struggle, yielded to affectionate sympathy, a feeling of warm solidarity with these independent and free people. The new style manifested itself not only in the colors; one of the characteristics of this new period, called the Rose Period, is a different handling of space: the figures are placed amid specific surroundings. They no longer appear in the blue infinity of a limitless void; they have their world. A whole series of canvases treats these circus or carnival subjects, among them the large painting *Family of Saltimbanques* (page 57) which inspired the opening lines of Rilke's fifth Duino Elegy; and the superb canvas at the Pushkin Museum in Moscow (figure 10), in which this idyllic and intimate feeling found its fullest expression. Now, the human contact between the figures becomes sympathetic: the

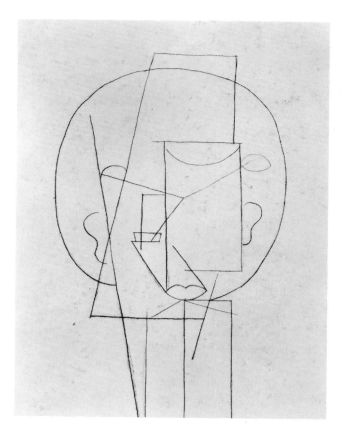

18. MALE HEAD. 1912–13. Drawing, charcoal on paper, 24⁵/₈ × 18³/₈″. *Private collection, New York*

tenderness of his new attitude toward life.

It is very possible that these first sculptures encouraged Picasso to study classical sculpture; the influence of the latter may be discerned in his drawings and watercolors of 1905 and early 1906. Alfred H. Barr, Jr., the most perceptive student of Picasso's art, used the term "First 'Classic' Period" to characterize these works. It is a fact that a concern with compositional values, volumes, and balance began to take precedence over the emotional content of his paintings (figure 10): the similarity between the bodies of his youths (for example, in *Boy Leading a Horse;* figure 8) and certain Greek *kouroi* in The Louvre can hardly be accidental. The study of Greek sculpture, the return to the Mediterranean classic tradition, must have had a peculiar significance in the work of Picasso. At the age of twenty-five, entering upon his maturity, he felt the need for objectivity, which from that moment on was to dominate his personal attitude. He borrowed a leaf from the anonymous tradition of pre-classical

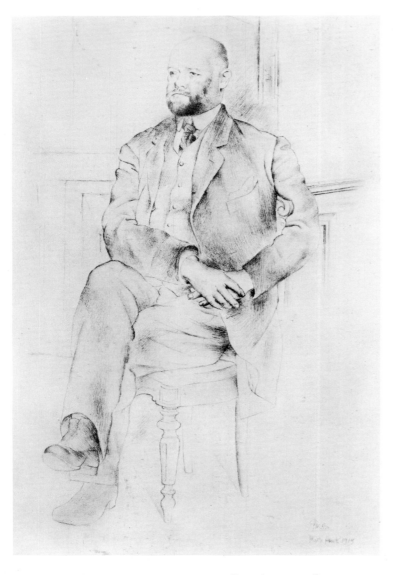

19. AMBROISE VOLLARD. 1915. Drawing, pencil on paper, $18^3/_8 \times 12^5/_8''$. *The Metropolitan Museum of Art, New York (Whittlesey Fund)*

morose atmosphere and loneliness of the Blue Period is a thing of the past. The authenticity of Picasso's feeling is shown by the fact that Rilke's poems about clowns, dating from the same time, express a similar emotion. The same attitude is seen in an important series of etchings, which date from 1904/5, but were published only several years later, in 1913, by Ambroise Vollard. After his trip to Holland Picasso also made his debut as a sculptor. His first work in this medium was a bust of a harlequin, and later a woman's head (figures 9, 15); many others were to follow at various periods of his life. These two early bronzes also reflect the calm and

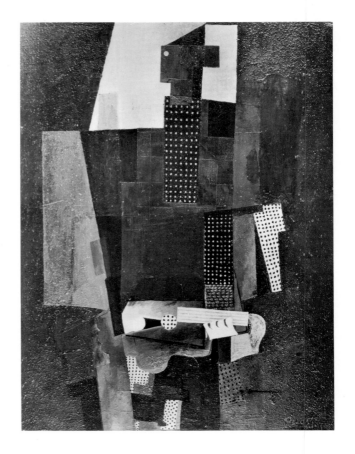

20. THE GUITAR PLAYER. 1916. Oil and sand on canvas, $51^1/_4 \times 38^1/_8''$. *Moderna Museet, Stockholm*

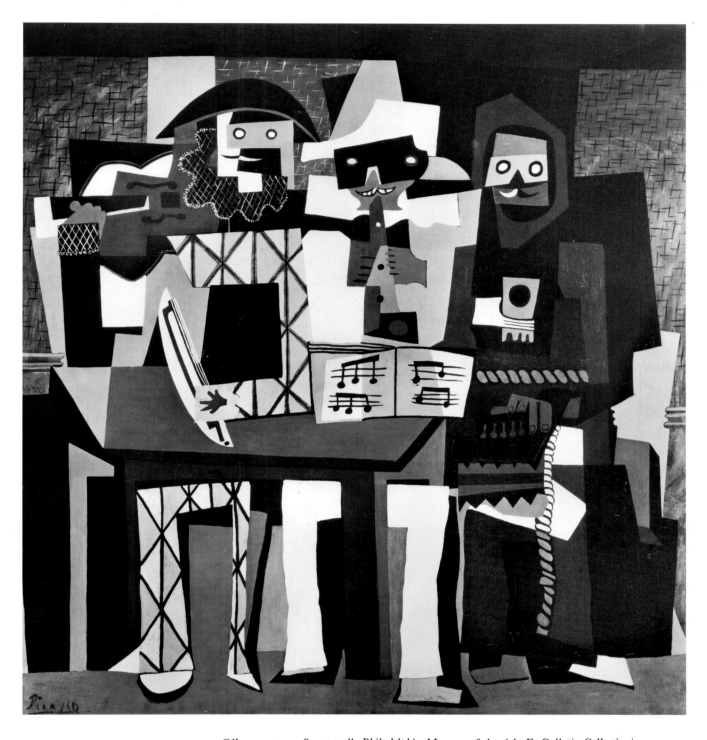

21. THREE MUSICIANS. 1921. Oil on canvas, 80 × 74″. *Philadelphia Museum of Art (A. E. Gallatin Collection)*

antiquity, in which he "found"—again his key word—an objective construction of forms and volumes, one that is not influenced by subjective feeling.

This tendency to objectivity, which was to dominate his work for almost twenty years, was further accentuated in 1906, as a result of a trip to Spain. As we have said, almost every change in

Picasso's art was inspired by renewed contact with his native land. He spent the summer of 1906 at Gosol in the Urgel valley, a primitive and rustic region in the foothills of the Pyrenees. Fernande Olivier was with him. There his "classic" style was transformed, taking on clearly primitive features: volume, sculptural effects became dominant. In the compositions of his

First "Classic" Period the figures were situated in a well-defined harmonious space; in the paintings that followed, in 1906, the volumes themselves create the space surrounding them, by the spatial energy of their plastic values. The portrait of Gertrude Stein marks the transition between the two periods (page 61). Begun early in 1906, it was not finished to the painter's satisfaction before his departure for Spain, although Miss Stein had sat for it eighty times. On his return from Gosol in the fall, Picasso painted the face from memory before seeing his model again. The portrait illustrates the difference between the two styles: the face, treated in a simplified manner, is an example of the new tendency.

The new monumental but compact style, which came to full flowering in the self-portrait painted early in 1907 (figure 12), may have been inspired by Picasso's interest in pre-Roman Iberian sculpture. Important examples of these had been discovered and published early in 1906,

and Picasso could have seen them in The Louvre. The simplified and suggestive construction of these heads, the elimination of all irrelevant detail, unquestionably find a parallel in Picasso's paintings of 1906. But it is impossible for a great artist's work to reflect an influence unless a tendency in that direction has already formed within him. Thus Picasso's study of Iberian and perhaps other primitive sculpture can only have urged along a disposition already manifested in his art—the tendency to simplification and greater objectivity of form, to suppression of detail, to a stronger spatial and plastic construction. The two self-portraits of 1906 and 1907, one in Philadelphia (page 63) and one in Prague, testify to the existence of this tendency in Picasso's painting, especially if it is seen as the continuation of the development begun with the face in the portrait of Gertrude Stein. This is the development that in 1907 led to Picasso's most important invention—Cubism.

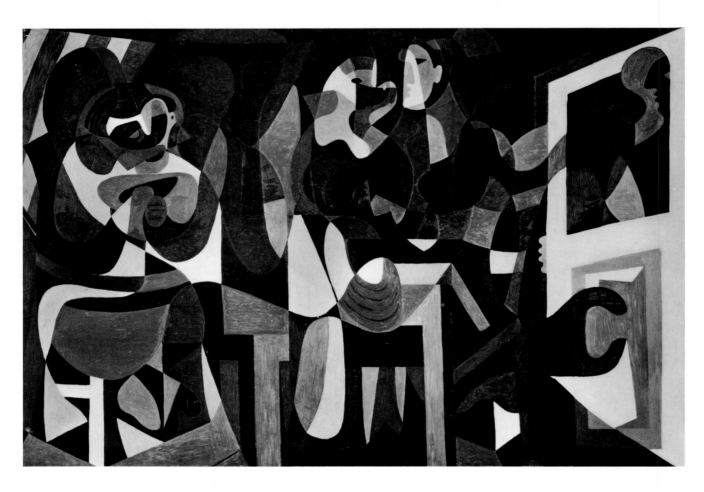

22. ATELIER OF THE MODISTE. 1926. Oil on canvas, $67^3/_4 \times 100^7/_8$". *Musée National d'Art Moderne, Paris*

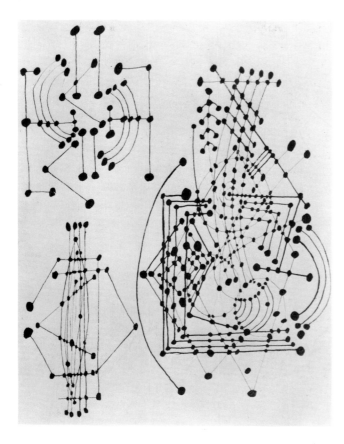

23. MUSICAL INSTRUMENTS. 1926. Drawing, India ink on paper, $12^3/_4 \times 9^3/_4''$. Illustration for Balzac, *Le Chef-d'œuvre inconnu*

* * *

The year 1907, a major turning point for Picasso and for all European painting, found the artist ensconced in a circle of friends. In 1906 he had met Henri Matisse (they remained close until Matisse's death); through Matisse he became a friend of André Derain and Georges Braque, both of whom belonged to the group known as Les Fauves, whose uncontested leader was Matisse. In 1907 he met Daniel-Henry Kahnweiler, who had recently opened a gallery at 28, Rue Vignon, and who became his loyal dealer, and an ardent and intelligent champion of Cubism.

The major event of 1907 for the art world was the retrospective exhibition of Cézanne, held at the Salon d'Automne, showing fifty-seven works by the painter who had gone beyond Impressionism through the discipline of his pictorial construction, and who had dreamed of making his art "a harmony parallel to nature." The need for objectivity that Cézanne had felt so strongly could not have failed to impress Picasso,

who was striving toward the same goal. However, the great canvas that marked his breakthrough to a new kind of painting, *Les Demoiselles d'Avignon* (page 65), had been virtually completed before the opening of the Cézanne exhibition. This disconcerting revolutionary work began a new direction in Picasso's painting; it also inaugurated a revolution in European painting, by its resolute abandonment of the traditional norms of classical beauty, by its deliberate barbarization of the human figure. It is the manifesto of the first revolt against sensory perception, of a new vision of the world.

The painting is not a complete unity; it was composed in two or even three stages, and the creative process can be clearly traced. It does not derive its importance from its artistic perfection,

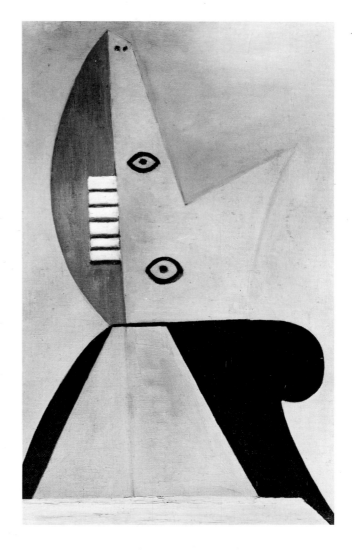

24. HEAD OF A YOUNG GIRL. 1929. Oil on canvas, $24 \times 15''$. *Kunstmuseum, Basel*

23

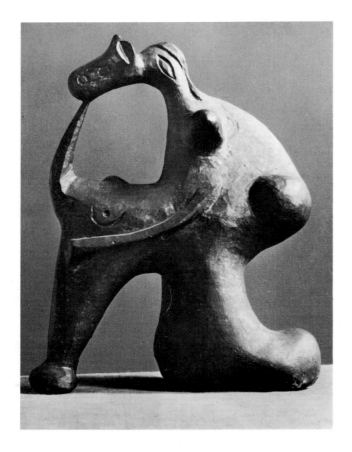

25. METAMORPHOSIS. 1928. Plaster, height 8⁷/₈″.
Musée Picasso, Paris

the picture obeys the same structural laws as the powerful, monumental torso of the figure: under the eyes of the artist who sought to synthesize his experiences, nature became one and indivisible. Body and space seem sculptured: the simple, strong design suggests an ax or a chisel, and it has nothing in common with the refinement that characterizes Picasso's early sculptures. The colors are reduced to tones of brown and ocher. In the landscapes of that year, which Picasso painted during a stay at La Rue-des-Bois (Oise), these colors are complemented by a saturated green, which brings out the simple harmony of the composition.

In these landscapes the influence of Cézanne is superimposed on the influence of Iberian and African sculpture. We see here a new style being worked out in close collaboration with Georges Braque. Braque's paintings—landscapes solidly constructed according to the precepts of Cézanne—after being rejected by the Salon d'Au-

but from its revolutionary qualities of boldness and shock. Traditional linear perspective is challenged, space is suggested by new means, traditional beauty is emphatically rejected: the painting is the result of a conception of the world that no longer rests upon sensory perception, but arises from a magical, intuitive feeling of life. It is a conception parallel to that of Bergson (whose *Creative Evolution* was published the same year); it is, in a word, a declaration of war against positivism, the philosophical system of bourgeois society, which is based upon total acceptance of perceptible reality, upon observation of facts.

Les Demoiselles d'Avignon is a point of departure; thereafter Picasso's path leads through hitherto unknown territory. In this monumental painting, space was already being treated as a solid substance, with a solidity equal to that of bodies and drapery. In the following year this painting was further unified, under the increased influence of Cézanne. In other works of the same period, such as the 1908 *Woman with a Fan,* everything in

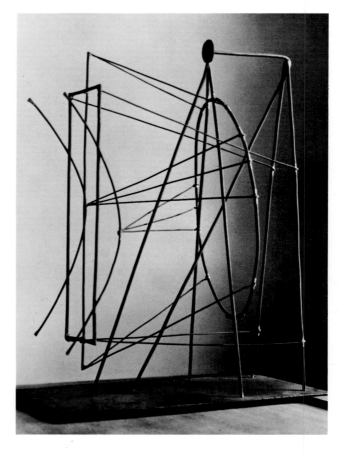

26. CONSTRUCTION. 1930. Iron wire, height 19⁷/₈″.
Musée Picasso, Paris

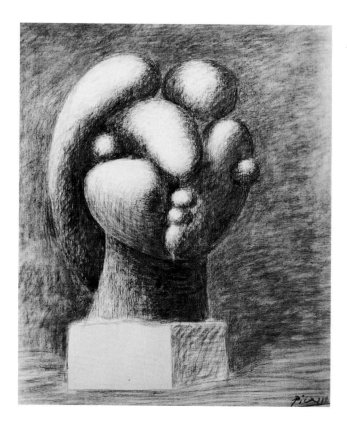

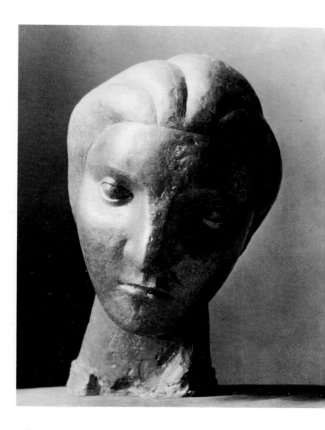

27. PROJECT FOR A SCULPTURE. 1932. Charcoal on canvas, 36¼ × 28¾″. *Galerie Beyeler, Basel*

28. HEAD OF A WOMAN. 1931–32. Bronze, height 22½′ *Collection the Artist's Estate*

tomne, were exhibited at Kahnweiler's. On that occasion a satirical reviewer coined the term "Cubism," which has since been used to designate this austere style. The year 1908 was also that of the famous banquet organized by Picasso in honor of the *douanier* Rousseau; this banquet too was an expression of the revolt of the group around Picasso against academic conventions, against a traditional conception of the world.

This rebellion was consolidated, once more, in Spain. Picasso spent the summer of 1909 at Horta de Ebro, and his stay in this bright and sunny countryside helped him solve his problem. He reduced his palette, confining himself to ochers and grays, and concentrated on the effects of volume. He proceeded "scientifically"—and the fact is significant—that is to say, by analysis. He reduced forms and volumes to their stereometric elements; renouncing chiaroscuro, he solidified space until it is suggested only through the angularity of the solids and their juxtaposition. The Horta landscapes—for instance, *The Reservoir at Horta de Ebro* (page 69)—are consistent

examples of this analytical vision of the world which aims at a systematic re-creation of reality. The purpose is no longer, as it was in Impressionist paintings, to evoke the fugitive charm of a sun-drenched landscape, but to discover it essential structure, to re-create it by a solid and disciplined architecture in accordance with the laws governing nature and the human mind. A bronze *Woman's Head* exemplifies the same structure as applied to the human figure (figure 15).

Analytic Cubism, as elaborated in the landscapes painted at Horta (together with several portraits and a group of still lifes), was perfected and carried further in the works of 1910, above all in the remarkable portraits of Uhde, of Vollard, and of Kahnweiler (page 71). Whereas in 1909 Picasso's aim had been to create a broad architecture in his painting, in 1910 the faceted perfect form of the crystal became the symbol of his art. Picasso now meticulously analyzed the forms, breaking them up into small structural planes; these were often rectilinear, like facets of a skillfully-cut diamond. This system of "overlapping planes"—which was applied both to the

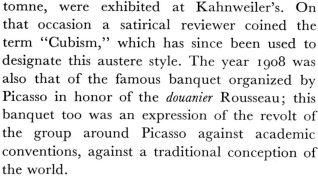

2

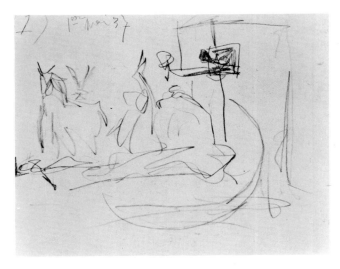

29. FIRST COMPOSITION STUDY FOR "GUERNICA." May 1, 1937.

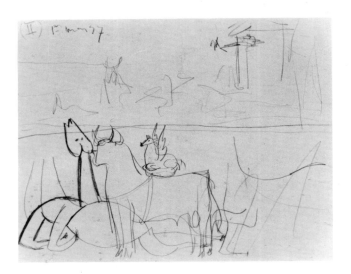

30. COMPOSITION STUDY FOR "GUERNICA." May 1, 1937.

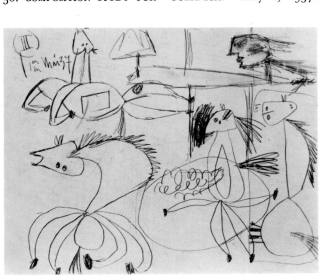

31. COMPOSITION STUDY FOR "GUERNICA." May 1, 1937.

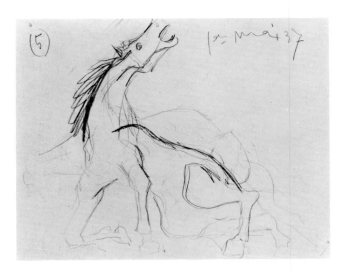

32. STUDY FOR A HORSE IN "GUERNICA." May 1, 1937.

Drawings on this page are in pencil on blue paper, $8^1/_4 \times 10^5/_8''$. *The Prado, Madrid*

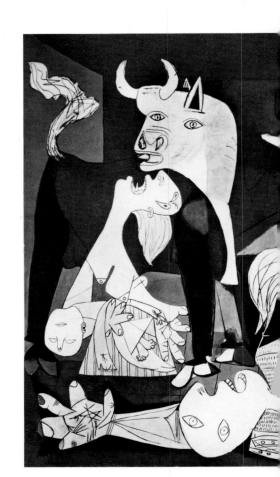

33. COMPOSITION STUDY FOR "GUERNICA." May 9, 1937. Drawing, pencil on white paper, $9^{1}/_{2} \times 17^{7}/_{8}''$.
The Prado, Madrid

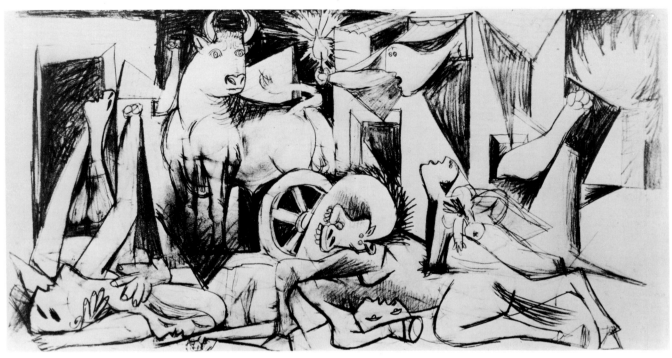

34. GUERNICA. 1937. Oil on canvas, 11'6'' × 25'8''. *The Prado, Madrid*

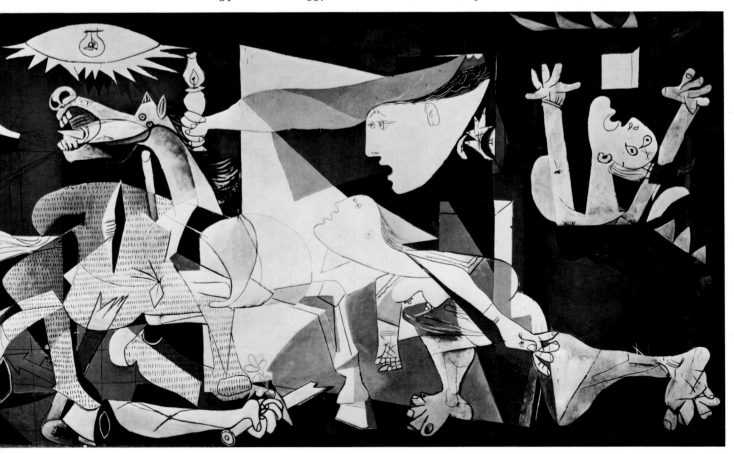

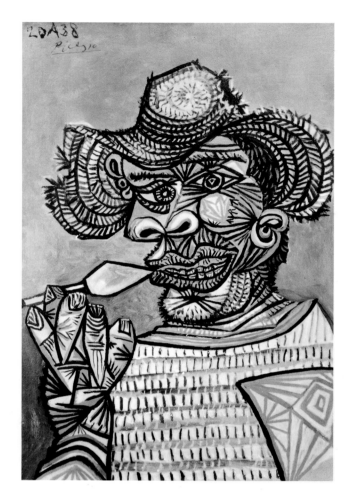

35. MAN WITH AN ALL-DAY SUCKER. 1938.
Oil on paper and canvas, 26⁷/₈ × 18″.
Collection Edward A. Bragaline, New York

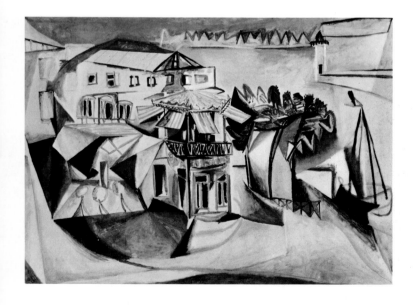

36. CAFE AT ROYAN. 1940. Oil on canvas, 38¹/₂ × 51¹/₄″.
Musée Picasso, Paris

figures and the surrounding space—endows these paintings with a tremendous eloquence: space is created by the viewer's eye just as, in earlier Impressionist paintings, tones were compounded in the viewer's eye by the juxtaposed spots.

These methodically and intricately calculated paintings of Picasso's are nonetheless lyrical; their lyricism has little surface charm, but a virile, controlled, and austere discipline that brings to mind Johann Sebastian Bach's *The Art of the Fugue.* The *Girl with Mandolin* (figure 16; painted shortly before the portraits) introduces this style, which acquires increasing precision, and reaches its apogee in the portrait of Kahnweiler. In 1911, during the summer which he spent in Céret (French Pyrenees) with Fernande Olivier and Braque, this direction was continued in a series of figures and still lifes and, later, in a sequence of etchings in the same sober and crystalline spirit, illustrating *Saint Matorel,* by his friend Max Jacob—the artist's first venture in book illustration. In the paintings, as in the etchings of this period, Picasso confined himself to a few nuances of gray by way of coloring; the brush strokes, visible until then, tended to disappear.

The disciplined objective Picasso achieved with this analysis of forms and volumes had become a language. Once the outlines of this language had been arrived at, he succeeded in simplifying its message in the works painted at L'Isle-sur-la-Sorgue (Vaucluse) in the summer of 1912. The large compositions, such as *The Aficionado,* are constructed out of simpler, less fragmented elements (page 75). At this stage, the implications of the Cubist revolution become apparent: the painter constructs a new world, beginning with geometric elements. He now entirely renounces the stationary point of view, which limits the apprehension of the object to an arbitrary angle of perception or viewpoint; he reconstitutes the object of his painting not on the basis of visual observation, but from his idea of it. Thus he creates a reality which transcends the arbitrary point of view of the accidental viewer, as well as the limited data of perception. This form of Cubism, which was born during the year 1913, is usually called Synthetic in opposition to the preceding Analytic phase.

In the emergence of this advanced style, a new

technique—collage—played a great part. In resorting to this technique, Picasso and Braque intended to achieve greater objectivity and impersonality. Braque took the first step in this direction when he introduced printed letters and surfaces painted to resemble wood or marble into his compositions, as a kind of trompe l'oeil. But the purpose was more than illusionistic: the

37. WOMAN WITH ORANGE. 1943. Bronze, height 70⁷/₈″. *Collection the Artist's Estate*

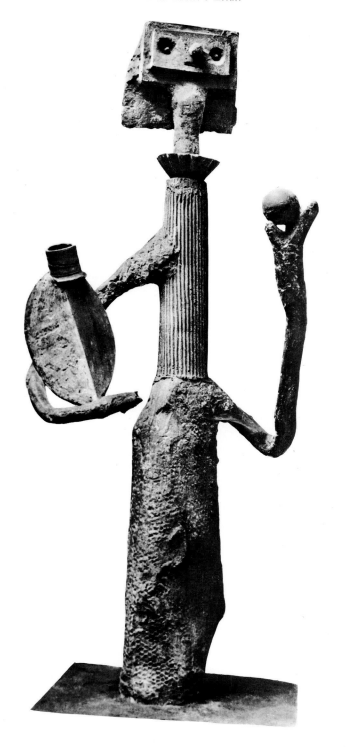

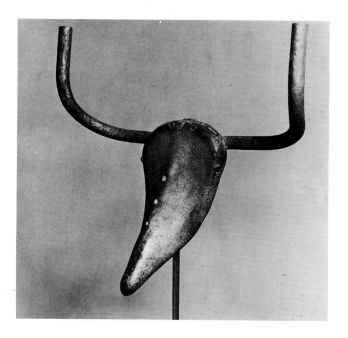

38. BULL'S HEAD. 1943. Handlebars and seat of a bicycle, height 13¹/₄″. *Musée Picasso, Paris*

two artists also tried to refer directly to reality in a way which, by contrast, would accentuate the artificiality of the painting. Medieval masters used the same technique when they emphasized the transcendent nature of their figures by placing real objects in their hands; and contemporary twentieth-century poets were moving in the same direction when they included in their poems conversations overheard in the streets. But in painting, this daring innovation has broader implications: having destroyed the unity of the object and the unity of space, the masters of Cubism set out to destroy the unity of the painted surface, the unity of the medium. By introducing "real details"—newsprint, colored paper, etc.—Picasso succeeds in creating signs bearing a new validity: he uses the new materials not as poetic metaphors, but to produce a true metamorphosis, a transfiguration. Some still lifes of 1913, for instance, *Bottle, Glass, and Violin* (page 77), and some heads, illustrate this: Picasso creates signs that represent reality instead of describing it. To give body to this new synthetic language, everyday things can serve, not as relevant objects, but as linguistic and syntactical examples. The technique of collage considerably influenced Picasso's easel paintings: his works of 1913, for example, *Woman in an Arm-*

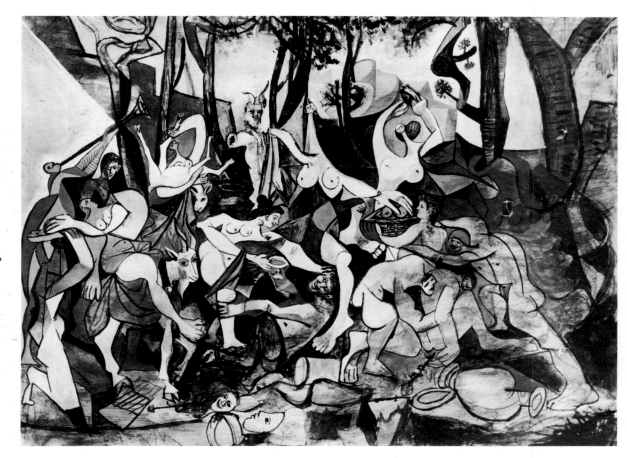

39. BACCHANAL,
after Poussin. 1944.
Watercolor and gouache,
12¼ × 16¼".
*Collection the Artist's
Estate*

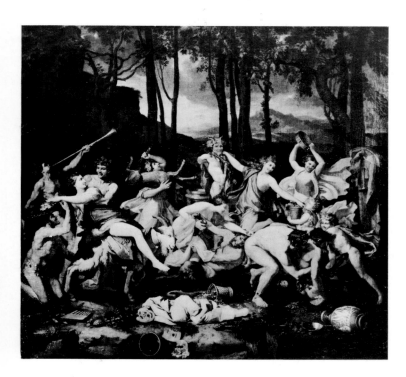

40. Nicolas Poussin: TRIUMPH OF PAN. 1638–39.
Oil on canvas, 54¾ × 61¾".
The Louvre, Paris (ex-Collection Jamot)

chair (page 79), demonstrate the change from an "analytic" to a "synthetic" structure of signs, resulting in a "conceptual painting," as Daniel-H. Kahnweiler calls it. In these works of 1913—*Card Player,* in the Museum of Modern Art, New York, and others—Picasso achieved monumental simplicity, a striking, definitive formula which was to be the basis of many of his subsequent works.

The outbreak of war in 1914 put an end to the collective adventure of Cubism: Braque and Derain, with whom Picasso had spent the summer at Avignon, left for their regiments; Picasso, alone of his group, could continue to work as an artist. His output of 1914 is characterized by a new gracefulness and lightness, which gave rise to Alfred H. Barr, Jr.'s, expression "Rococo" Cubism. Whereas the works of the preceding period bring to mind the austerity of Bach's music, those of 1914 (for instance, *Portrait of a Girl*) suggest Mozart's graceful trills: the "dot" or *pointilliste* treatment, the boa around the shoulders, and a number of other details contribute above all to a reestablishment of color—a development which had been foreshadowed in 1913. Because his friends had been called to war, Picasso was now the only painter to develop this phase of Cubism in the following years, reaching another high point in *The Guitar Player* of 1916 (figure 20), and terminating in 1921 with the two versions of *Three Musicians* (figure 21; page 85), incontestable masterpieces, convincing in their clarity.

As we have said, Cubism, the collective attempt at a style characteristic of our time, came to an end in 1914. Although Picasso continued it during the war years, even for him this language, this image of the world (which Cubism is) lost its exclusive validity. In 1915, to the astonishment of his friends, he made two portrait drawings—one of Max Jacob and one of Ambroise Vollard (figure 19)—in a meticulously realistic style. He had not used this style since 1906, and to do a painting based on the data of sensory perception had seemed out of the question after the revolutionary breakthrough of Cubism. Why then did he go back to the old conception of reality which he himself had discarded? Was it because the chaos of the war—the overwhelming concern of all his friends—could not be expressed in the precise and methodical language of Cubism? Or was it because the development of a supra-personal style required after all a collective effort, which was a task beyond the strength of one individual, no matter how gifted and imaginative? Whatever the case may be, since 1915 realistic styles have existed side by side with Cubism in Picasso's work. From that moment on Picasso was committed to no single style, and used many different approaches to express his ideas and feelings.

The first evidence of this newly acquired freedom came in 1917. At the invitation of Jean Cocteau, Picasso went to Rome to execute the stage designs and costumes for Cocteau's ballet, *Parade*. His drawings and sets reveal for the first time the coexistence of various styles and modes of expression. The curtain was painted in a joyously realistic manner, while the costumes—at least those of the fantastic figures of the "managers"—were rigorously Cubist. This juxtaposition was unheard-of in theatrical art. Picasso's friends

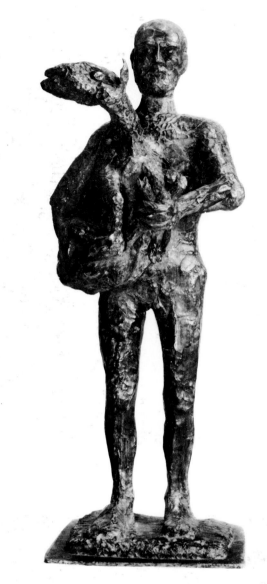

41. SHEPHERD CARRYING A LAMB. 1944. Bronze, height 86⅝". *Philadelphia Museum of Art (Gift of R. Sturgis and Marion B. F. Ingersoll)*

were amazed when it occurred also in his painting: the same year produced the portrait of Olga Koklova (who later became Picasso's wife), a meticulously realistic work, worthy of the great nineteenth-century masters such as Ingres; and the severely Cubist canvas, *Italian Woman*. The two styles continued to overlap during the following years, in works in which the human figure, treated in one style or the other, gained increasing importance. This fact is partly accounted for by Picasso's work in the ballet: clowns, dancers, and other such figures played a greater part in his life than even during the Rose Period.

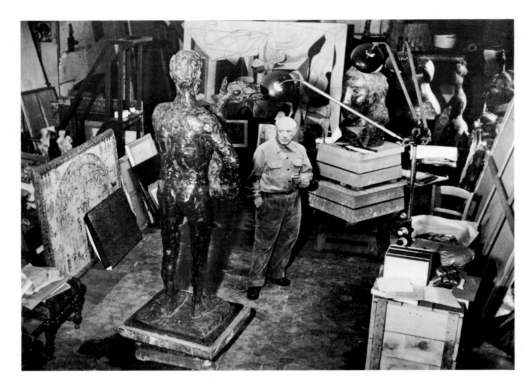

The world of the ballet which inspired a series of drawings and canvases finds its apotheosis in the two versions of *Three Musicians*, the highest expression of Synthetic Cubism (figure 21; page 85). The two versions differ in composition, color, and even in the general feeling of the visual structure; taken together, they constitute a definitive statement of the creative discoveries of Cubism, which they put to full use: simple and geometrically defined forms constitute signs which, by means of this deliberate and enchanting metamorphosis, take on life and a surprising suggestiveness.

At the opposite pole of Picasso's artistic creation, another series of canvases began to take shape simultaneously: the cycle of heads and figures inspired by classical antiquity. This was continued after 1921 in paintings treating the theme of mother and child. As early as 1920 the influence of Roman sculpture was apparent in these enormous heads and gigantic figures. It reflected the return to antiquity, to tradition, which prevailed in every intellectual area during the first years after the war and was symptomatic of a general reaction against chaos and destruction, and of the attempt to rebuild European culture after the four disastrous years. The music of Stravinsky, Italian painting, poetry through-

out Europe—all were part of that movement. But in Picasso's work, another motive intervened, which was to reappear about ten years later—the need to create a mythology for himself.

In 1918 Picasso married Olga Koklova, prima ballerina of the Ballets Russes for which he had worked in Rome. In 1921 their son Paul was born. It was after this that the subject of mother and child, mentioned above, reappears as a major theme in the guise of monumental figures devoid of personal allusion, transported into a realm of mythology (page 89). The painting of 1923 is a telling example of this, doubly remarkable for the restraint of its color (for it is contemporaneous with brilliantly colored works). And just as the mythical figures of the Blue Period had yielded to the emotional compositions of the Rose Period, these gigantic figures of a mythological universe gave way to tender portraits of the young Paul. The painting of Paul sketching, with the blue sky seen through the window behind him, fully expresses the artist's love for his son.

In 1924 we find the opposite pole again predominant: that year began the great series of still lifes, in which Picasso magnificently displayed his feeling for composition and arrangement. He made use of the same simple, everyday objects

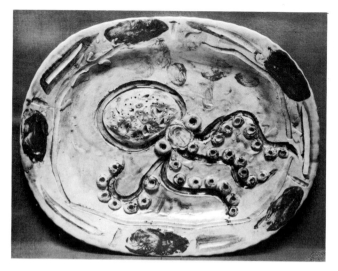

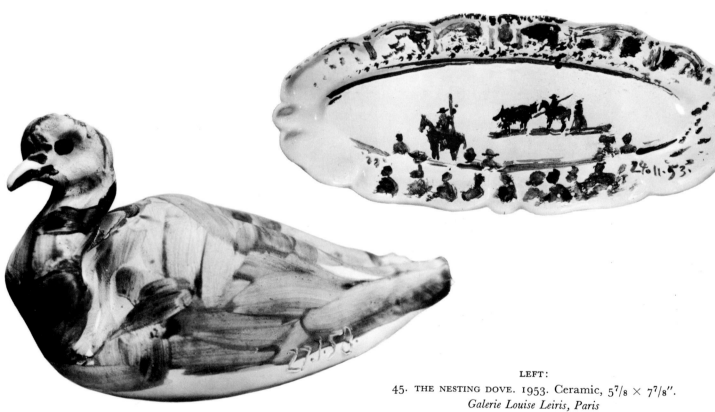

he had used once before in the Cubist period—the violin, the guitar, bottles, a bar. But the forms of the objects are now ample and sumptuous, and the bright colors confer upon them a radiant splendor. In addition to these recapitulations of old themes in a new guise, Picasso returned to the theme of the woman with mandolin (which he had treated as early as 1910) in one of his most harmonious compositions of that time, dated 1925 (page 93).

The same year showed the most surprising divergence in Picasso's art: side by side with the balanced Apollonian masterpiece *Woman with Mandolin* (page 93), he painted *Three Dancers*, a major example of the Dionysiac and obsessed strain in his art, in contrast. Everything in this work—the exaggerated gestures, the fantastic distribution of the limbs of the human body, the distortions—suggests what Rimbaud called "the derangement of the senses," intoxication, ecstasy.

Picasso denied that he had been influenced by Surrealism (as had been claimed, on the basis of this painting); and yet it is obvious that he was affected by the state of mind which, around 1925, reflected a loss of faith in the attempts to create order, and which sought salvation in the irrational. In this painting Picasso went further than the Surrealists, and expressed the Dionysiac aspect of life with unprecedented ardor, at the same time adding a new facet to the richness of his work.

However, this Dionysiac strain reappeared only intermittently. In 1925 Picasso painted a large composition of figures, *Atelier of the Modiste* (figure 22), which is diametrically opposed to the unbridled ecstasy of *Three Dancers*. Executed in subdued grays, transected by curves in the manner of a jigsaw puzzle, this work suggests calm and order. In 1926 Picasso also produced a number of enigmatic drawings which seem abstract; actually the points and lines form an orderly system, inspired by maps of the sky.

The obsessed, hallucinatory aspect of his work reappears in 1927: the curves of *Atelier of the Modiste* are used in a different way in the *Seated Woman*, to produce an eloquent expression of anguish which is further underlined by the strident color composition. Then the Dionysiac strain of 1925 reappears in the small canvases painted at Dinard on the English Channel during the summer of 1928. The lively figures of the bathers in striped swimming suits express a similar arbitrary fantasy, in unexpected contrast with the systematic fragmentation of shapes during the Cubist period. Magical feeling has outstripped intellectual discipline, whose basic concept had proved illusory and utopian in contemporary history. The *Projects for Monuments* dating from around 1929 most strikingly reveal the anguished and obsessed side of Picasso's art. They show heads of women, conceived as monumental sculptures (they were supposedly intended for the Promenade at Cannes, as symbols of a demonic spirit; figure 27). These "architectural metamorphoses" are reminiscent of Surrealism, but differ from it nonetheless, because in Picasso's art the element of shock, of surprise, lies not in the objects themselves, but in the quality of the forms. The works of those years reflect a consciousness of all impulses as demonic, an aware-

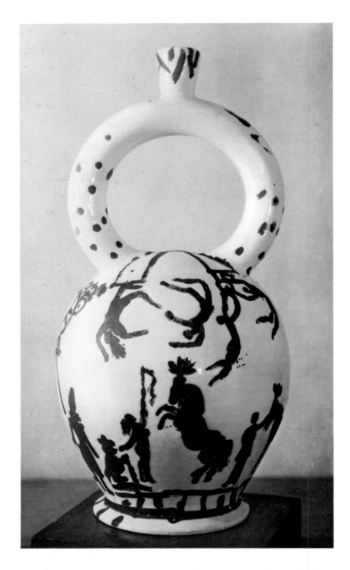

46. THE CIRCUS VASE. 1954. Ceramic, height 22⁷/₈″.
Galerie Louise Leiris, Paris

ness of a threat underlying the artist's conception of the world.

At the end of the decade, these metamorphoses were the dominant theme in paintings and small sculptures with ambiguous forms. It is perhaps no accident that in 1930 Picasso felt drawn to illustrate Ovid's *Metamorphoses:* he executed thirty etchings of the story in a flexible and classical linear style, with strongly disciplined form—a true shorthand of the line. With these works he resumed his activity as an illustrator; at the same time they mark the beginning of an attempt to create for himself a new and authentic mythology. During the same year he painted a small *Crucifixion*—this too pointing to the artist's need to express preoccupations of a general or even intimately personal kind in the form of timeless symbols. This need inspired his print-making and, during the following years, his sculpture; the many attempts in this direction culminated in the monumental *Guernica* of 1937.

In 1930 Picasso purchased the Château du Bois-geloup, near Gisors (Eure). In 1931 he set up a studio there and, with the help of his friend Julio González, executed a number of sculptures (figures 26, 28). The large heads of women of a pervasive calm are related to the paintings from 1932 and subsequent years representing a seated or reclining blonde woman absorbed in a blissful dream; the drawing is marked by harmonious curves, and the colors are primary and brilliant. The model for these paintings was Marie-Thérèse Walter, who, in 1935, gave birth to his daughter Maia. This series of works was continued until 1935 (during the "season in hell" which he went through because of his separation from Olga Koklova) in the paintings such as *Young Woman Drawing* (page 107). In them, a feeling of quiet is dominant over the artist's personal troubles and the anxieties caused by the state of the world at the time.

These anxieties constitute the undercurrent of his activities in the 1930s; they account for his attempts to create a modern mythology. After the great retrospective exhibitions of his work in Paris and Zurich, 1932, Picasso began to treat mythological themes. The cycle had begun with Ovid's great poem *Metamorphoses* of 1930 and it continued with his illustrations for Aristophanes' *Lysistrata* in 1934. In the same year, on a long visit to Spain, he came upon a new means of satisfying his need to create mythological signs expressing the obsessions of our epoch: the theme of tauro-machy—the bullfight—which had been familiar to him since his youth. As so often before, it was the contact with Spain that had brought into focus this new style, this freshly acquired aspect of his art. The bull appeared for the first time in some sketches of 1934, as the plastic sign of demon-possessed fury. In 1935, the mysteri-ous, masterful etching *Minotauromachy* introduced the enigmatic figure of Picasso's Minotaur. In 1936 these mythological attempts acquired a poignant basis in reality: civil war broke out in

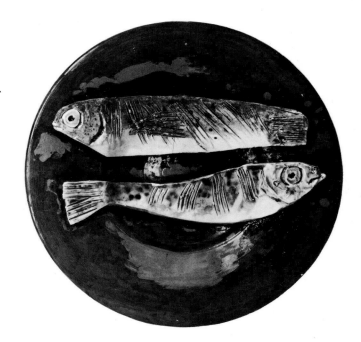

47. FISH. 1957. Ceramic relief, diameter 16⁷/₈″.
Galerie Louise Leiris, Paris

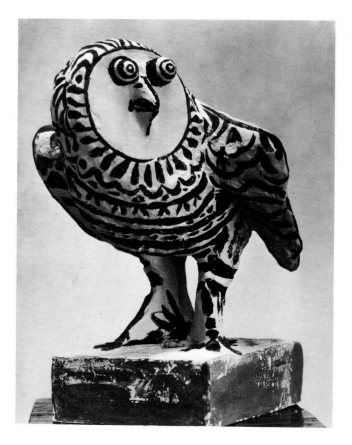

48. THE WHITE OWL. 1952. Ceramic, height 13″.
Galerie Louise Leiris, Paris

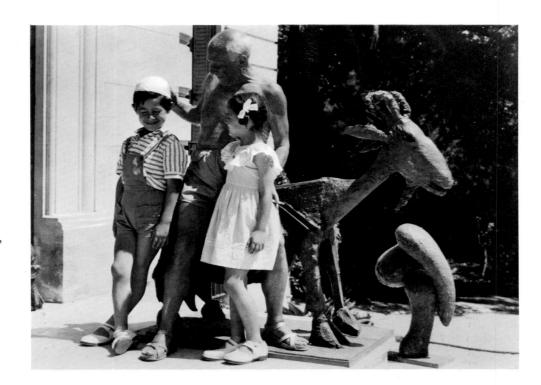

49. Picasso with his children,
Claude and Paloma, 1957

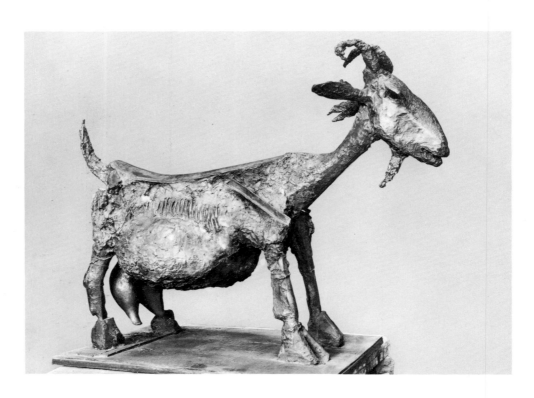

50. GOAT. 1950. Bronze,
$46^3/8 \times 56^3/8''$.
*The Museum of Modern Art,
New York (Mrs. Simon
Guggenheim Fund)*

Spain, where Picasso's work had been exhibited in the spring under the sponsorship of his friend Paul Eluard. Picasso wholeheartedly embraced the republican cause, and was appointed director of The Prado. Early in 1937 he composed his first work dealing with the civil war, a series of etchings entitled *The Dream and Lie of Franco*. He was commissioned to paint a large canvas for the Spanish Republic's pavilion at the Paris World's Fair that was to open in the summer of 1937. He had not yet begun it when he was roused by the news of the bombing, on April 28, 1937, of the small, unprotected town of Guernica, by German planes in the service of Franco. By May

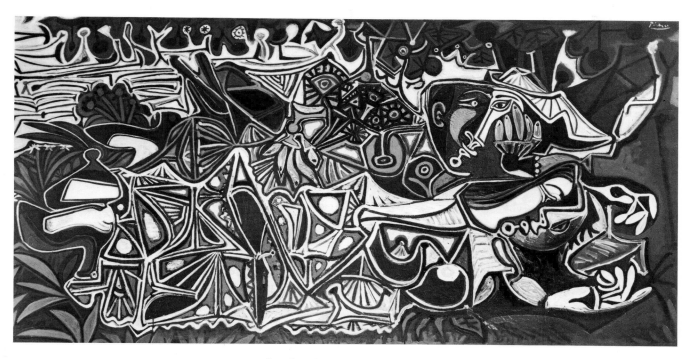

51. WOMEN ON THE BANKS OF THE SEINE, after Courbet. 1950. Oil on plywood, 39⅝ × 79⅛″. *Kunstmuseum, Basel*

ı he was making the first sketches for the immense canvas which marks the high point of his mythological creations, and which is one of the masterpieces of twentieth-century painting, its most distilled, most passionate expression (figures 29–32).

A long series of sketches followed those of May ı (figure 33); the composition was completed early in June. The principal elements were present in the first sketch and took definitive form in the drawing of May 9. The subsequent work led to a condensation, however, a more effective concentration of the signs; the final version brings together within the austere framework of a triangular composition, the bull, the horse, the woman with the lamp—motifs used previously in the *Minotauromachy*. But the meaning, the emotional expressiveness of the signs, has become more tense and explosive: the horse and the bull are graven more deeply on the viewer's memory than are the human figures; thus it is the mythological signs of suffering and ruthless brute force that dominate the work. In this great painting Picasso created a poignant monument against barbarian aggressive force; though it contains no allusion to the specific event for which it is named, it constitutes a warning to mankind against the implications of unleashing the forces of darkness. History proved Picasso right: Warsaw, Rotterdam, Coventry, Smolensk, and Hiroshima are stations along the road which began at Guernica.

In addition to *Guernica*, the year 1937 was filled with works that the critic Alfred H. Barr, Jr., called "postscripts" to *Guernica*—canvases in which

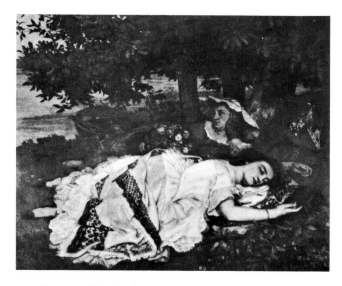

52. Gustave Courbet: LES DEMOISELLES AUX BORDS DE LA SEINE. 1856. Oil on canvas, 19¼ × 20⅞″.
Petit Palais, Paris

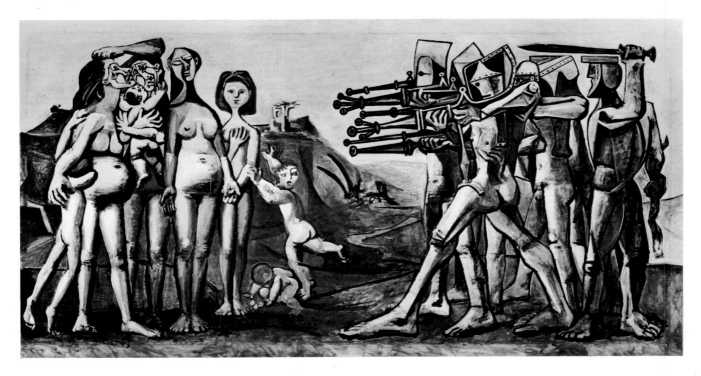

53. MASSACRE IN KOREA. 1951. Oil on canvas, 43$^1/_4$ × 82$^1/_2$″. *Musée Picasso, Paris*

the same feelings of rage, indignation, and impotent revolt were expressed in the faces of women, as in *Weeping Woman;* in these the suffering and distress are manifested dramatically, in a manner that goes beyond the anecdotal (page 109). This strain continued in 1938 with several heads of men crowned with thorns, with tor-

mented expressions, painted at Mougins during the summer. But this dramatic and tragic series was counterbalanced by a series of aquatints dating from the same period, illustrating Buffon's *Histoire naturelle;* these were executed in a flexible, realistic style, and enriched by subtly graduated grays.

54. Francisco Goya:
THE THIRD OF MAY,
1808. 1814–15.
Oil on canvas,
104$^3/_4$ × 135$^5/_8$″.
The Prado, Madrid

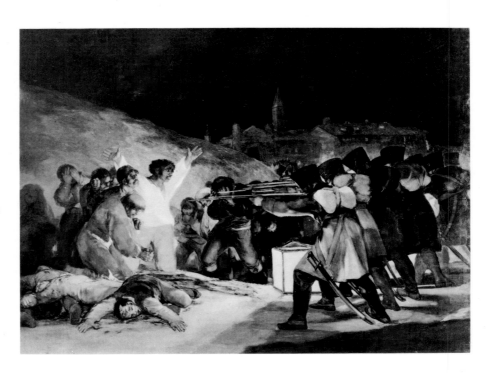

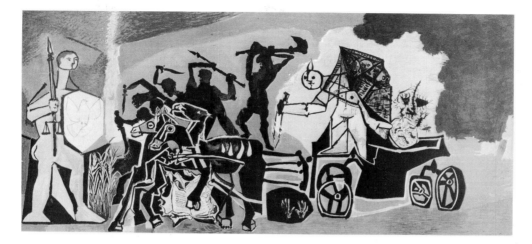

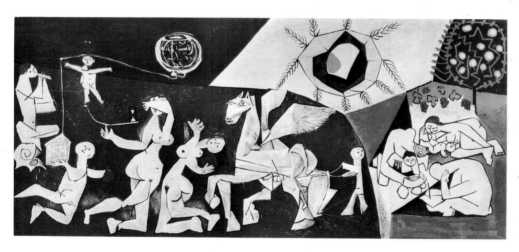

In 1939 a large number of Picasso's canvases were brought to the United States for a retrospective exhibition organized in New York by The Museum of Modern Art. During the months preceding the declaration of the Second World War Picasso worked at Antibes. The little Mediterranean port provided the background for the masterpiece of that period, *Night Fishing at Antibes* —a nocturne in stained-glass-window colors—in which the peaceful details at the periphery clash with the ferocity of the scene at the center, unconsciously symbolizing the months of suspense that preceded the outbreak of the world conflict.

After war was declared Picasso left Antibes for Paris, where he stayed only a few days, and then went to Royan, a fishing village and summer resort at the mouth of the Gironde. It was there that he painted one of his most terrifying works— *Nude Dressing Her Hair*, a hard, sculptural work which rises like a true sphinx, enigmatic and

frightening. But even this anguished creation was counterbalanced by graceful, pleasing paintings from the same year, 1940, such as *Café at Royan*, done in bright and sparkling colors (figure 36).

However, the atmosphere of anguish expressed in *Nude Dressing Her Hair* was to haunt Picasso's work during the war years, which he spent in Paris, shut up in his studio in the Rue des Grands-Augustins. His obsessions were expressed primarily in paintings of the half-figure of a woman seated in an armchair in a small room. *Seated Woman in Blue* (1944; Musée National d'Art Moderne, Paris) is an eloquent example, one of the least aggressive: the color harmony is in deliberate contrast with the attitude of the figure, which is, so to speak, imprisoned by the arms of the armchair. In this and the other paintings of the series, a plastic device recurs continually: the fusion of the profile with the front view of the face. This suggestive artifice originated in the Cubism of the years around 1914 (*Italian Woman*

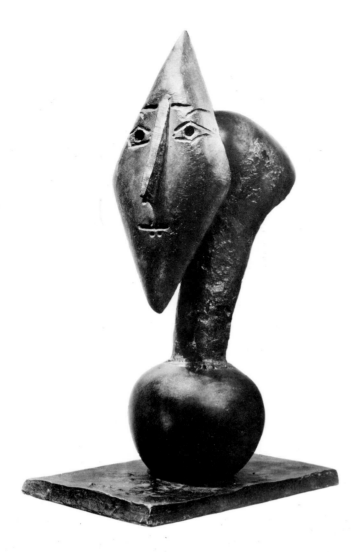

was also expressed during the war years, in still lifes, in sculptures, and in poetry. In 1941, Picasso wrote a Surrealist play, *Desire Trapped by the Tail*, which was performed by a group of friends in the apartment of the Leirises in 1944. In it we find the same authenticity of invention which enchantingly metamorphoses objects into human figures. The same may be said of the *Bull's Head*, made with the handlebars and seat of a bicycle combined in a new, suggestive manner (figure 38).

With the liberation of Paris (August 25, 1944), a profound change took place in Picasso's life. He emerged from his wartime isolation as the universally acclaimed master, the symbol of the artist who had succeeded in outwitting the brutality and cunning of the Nazi occupiers. The day of liberation found him busy making a free copy of a *Bacchanal* by Poussin, *Triumph of Pan*

58. BABOON AND YOUNG. 1951. Bronze, height 21″.
The Museum of Modern Art, New York
(Mrs. Simon Guggenheim Fund)

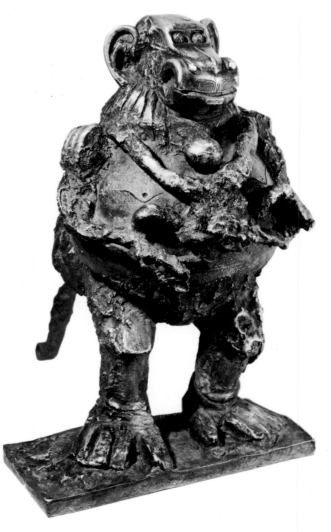

57. HEAD OF A WOMAN. 1951. Bronze, height 21¹/₈″.
The Museum of Modern Art, New York
(Benjamin and David Scharps Fund)

of 1917 is one of the earliest examples), reappeared in the series of dreaming women of 1932, and then became more frequent from 1937 on. It is a mode of definition which began with the delineation of inanimate objects in the Cubist period, and was applied to the human figure after the latter had assumed a central expressive value in Picasso's painting. His *Woman with Fish Hat*, the other example from the wartime series, combines a satire on food rationing (the hat with the fish, quarter of a lemon, knife and fork) with the obsessive pose of the figure, hands clenched, in an empty and hallucinated space (page 113). The faces and figures of the women are evidence of an immensely inventive intensity; they are plastic symbols, always different and always expressive, for a wide variety of states of mind of the artist. His self-contained inner life

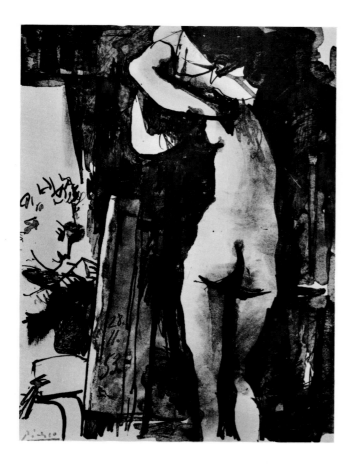

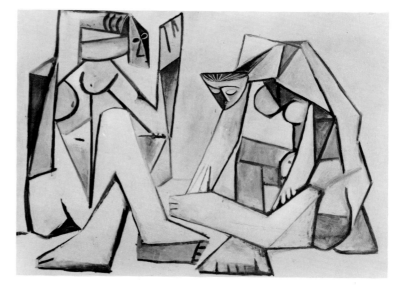

59. MODEL UNDRESSING. 1953. Drawing, ink on paper, 9³/₈ × 7". *Private collection, Stockholm*

(figures 39, 40)—the first of his adaptations of old master paintings. But his reply to the years of oppression was manifested not only in paintings: his joining the French Communist Party was also part of this reply. This political act by a man whose art had largely kept clear of politics was indirectly connected with his feeling of solidarity with the poor, with his social attitude during the period of *Arte Joven* in Madrid, in 1901. The bronze sculpture *Shepherd Holding a Lamb* (figures 41, 62), a secular variation on the theme of the Good Shepherd, expresses this theme in modern terms, suitable to 1944.

The world of art displayed the greatest admiration for Picasso. At the Salon de la Libération, held in the fall of 1944, a large hall was reserved for his works—seventy-four paintings and five sculptures. This was the first time Picasso had taken part in the Salon d'Automne, and it was the first time his enormous production from the war years had been shown to the public. But in the years following his wartime isolation he

produced works of a new sort—views of Paris painted in tribute to the heroic city, composed like stained-glass windows of bits of color framed in thick black lines. The same style, inspired by stained-glass windows, with their emphatic contours, characterizes the still lifes of 1945; the most outstanding example is *Still Life with Pitcher, Candle, and Enamel Pot* (page 115). And that year, side by side with this monumental style, Picasso began to develop an entirely free and occasionally playful art in his lithographs. The series of variations on the theme of the Bull shows him capable of developing a form taken from nature to the point where it is reduced to a bare sign.

In 1946 Picasso found a new climate of life on the Mediterranean coast, which led to a rejuvenation in his art: he discovered there a cheerful paganism, the idyllic carefree spirit of ancient mythology. This gave rise to a series of paintings and lithographs peopled with fauns, centaurs, and ancient figures, culminating in the large composition *La Joie de vivre*, a mythological apotheosis of a life relaxed in the sun, symbol of a harmony rediscovered after years of the war's terror. This whole joyous world came into being at the museum of Antibes, whose curator put at Picasso's disposal the spacious halls of the Palais Grimaldi. And this world of fauns and bacchantes continued in the work of Picasso, but in a new ambiance: it spills over from

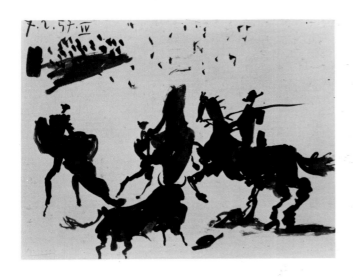

61. BULLFIGHT. 1957. Drawing, ink on paper,
19¾ × 25¾". *Formerly Galerie Louise Leiris, Paris*

painting into ceramics. Picasso discovered pottery in 1946, thanks to Suzanne and Georges Ramié, managers of the Madoura factory in Vallauris. He moved there in October, 1947, and devoted himself to ceramics for almost a year. In that period he produced works of the most varied kinds—dishes lightly painted, platters on which this mythological world appears, as well as vases which, thanks to the magic of his imagination, were metamorphosed into owls, women, or heads of fauns (figures 43–48). This feverish activity was interrupted by only one trip, to Poland, to attend the Congress for Peace—an act of faith which coincided with his regained optimism. In 1949 he drew for the same Congress, held that year in Paris, his dove of peace, to fly across the world.

After his work in ceramic, Picasso began to explore a territory on which he had set foot only a little earlier: the "translation" of the paintings of old masters. After painting his variation on the theme of Poussin's *Bacchanal* on the day of the liberation, he took Courbet's *Girls on the Banks of the Seine* as his subject in 1950 (figures 51, 52), and later that year, El Greco's *Portrait of a Painter*. These works are actual translations of classics into Picasso's language and style. But events in the outside world did not permit him to continue this confrontation with works of his choice: the Korean war broke out, and he felt obliged once more to raise his voice against barbarism: he painted the *Massacre in Korea* (figure

53). He was faced once again with the dilemma between harmony and horror, a fact attested by his two big compositions, *War* and *Peace* (figures 55, 56). The distressing, torn aspect of his art reappeared after so many years, for instance, in the still life *Goat's Skull, Bottle, and Candle*, which contrasts so bitterly with his sculpture of a goat, a subtle and moving work by a magician of forms (figure 50).

In the course of the next ten years, we find an alternation between two themes and two styles: on the one hand, the affectionate, uninhibited signs of his personal life (figure 49), on the other, the confrontation with the works of old masters. The first category includes works such as *The Meal* of 1953, whose subject is his two youngest children, Claude and Paloma, with their mother; the rich and varied series of portraits of Sylvette (1954) which transforms the head of a girl with a pony-tail into an emblem; more recent works, like *The Studio* of 1956, which distills the sundrenched space of his villa's big studio at Cannes into an arabesque; and finally the still life of 1959, in which the old furniture of his new residence at Vauvenargues becomes the symbol of the peaceful calm of the house. Between these works and the "translations" there is inserted a brutal and disturbing painting, *Two Women on the Beach* (figure 60), which brings to mind again his disquieting fantasies of the years around 1928. On the other hand, his dialogue with the old masters continued to be enriched. In 1955 he began a series of fifteen variations on Delacroix' *Femmes d'Alger*; in 1957 he tackled the *Maids of Honor (Las Meninas)* by Velázquez; and in 1960/61 he had his confrontation with Manet's *Déjeuner sur l'herbe* (page 125). These translations are not mere stylistic exercises, they are like true "musical variations," comparable to the magnificent variations which composers create from the themes of other composers: they served to strengthen Picasso's own authentic, personal style. He displayed in them an incomparable freedom—a freedom that only one who is the equal of the great painters can permit himself. Thus, by his own free will, he rejoined the chain of the great masters, in which he deserves a place by his mastery, his richness, and his authenticity.

This mastery was convincingly proven anew by the large, simultaneous exhibitions organized in

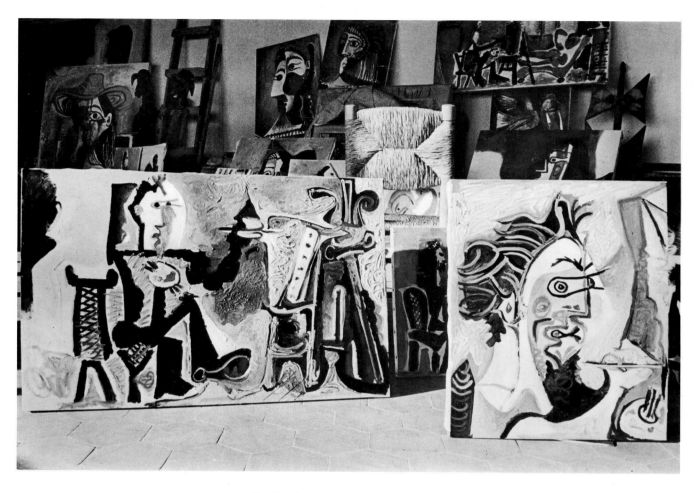

62. In the studio at Mougins, 1963

1966 by the Paris museums to celebrate Picasso's eighty-fifth birthday. For the first time, all visitors could appreciate the consistent and impressive stream of paintings, sculptures, and prints he had produced—from his earliest years, to the most recent series of the *Painter at His Easel,* his graphic works, and the latest prints (the aquatints he produced for Pierre Reverdy's *Sable mouvant*).

By 1968, Picasso had begun to concentrate more and more upon graphic works: in that year, between March and October, he completed *Suite 347,* comprising 347 etchings based mainly on erotic themes—the eroticism of an old man still aflame with passion and joie de vivre. The first page of the *Suite* (figure 63), shows the artist as a regisseur of his own theater, of the world he has created. And the next year, Picasso again provided proof of his mastery as a painter and a creator of stirring images with a series of about 140 canvases, among which such works as *The Kiss* display his vitality and the consistency of his later, almost Baroque style. This series was

exhibited in 1970 in the Palace of the Popes in Avignon, and that same year, the artist donated a large number of his early works to the Picasso Museum in Barcelona.

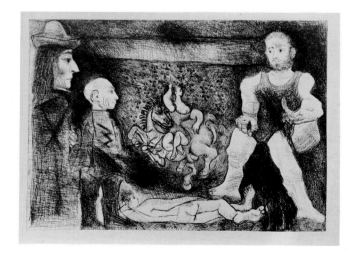

63. PAGE I OF SUITE 347. 1973. Etching. *Musée Picasso, Paris*

43

The artist's ninetieth birthday, in 1971, was the occasion for an exhibition of his selected works at the Grande Galerie of The Louvre—Picasso was the first living artist to be thus honored. But this exhibition was by no means a mere commemoration: Picasso continued to work, mainly in drawings (figure 64) and prints, with unflagging energy. And there are paintings completed in 1972 which exemplify his characteristic independence, as well as the continuity of his work. Only his death on April 8, 1973, at the age of ninety-one, could halt this amazing flow of creative mastery in painting, sculpture, and the graphic arts.

No one will doubt Picasso's mastery. But his richness, the variety of his work, never ceases to confound even the lovers of his painting. His enormous virtuosity, his ability to do whatever he wants to, contributes to the bewilderment of viewers: they see no connection, no coherence, between works as remote from one another as are the faithful and lovingly naturalistic portraits on the one hand, and the fantastic monsters on the other. The opinion is sometimes expressed that a historian of the future, confronted with Picasso's work in the absence of any documentation, could never believe that all this was created by one man, one mind.

And yet it is this seemingly so disparate creativity that constitutes Picasso's authenticity, his contribution to painting, to art in general. He refused to be frozen into a historical monument by practicing only one style, making that his specialty: he would have called such self-limitation a betrayal of life. Nor did he aspire to the absolute perfection of the masterpiece. "In former times," he said, "paintings approached perfection by degrees. Every day added something new. A painting was the result of additions. For me, the painting is the result of destructions. I make a painting, then I destroy it. But in the end nothing has been lost." He rejected perfection, the consummation of a picture, because he attached too much importance to variety, to the flexibility of life. He might have entered history as the great master of Cubism, or even of the melancholy realism of the Blue Period—but he refused to do so. In his boundless faith in life he refused to let his art be frozen into styles or laws; he believed only in authenticity, the undiluted expression of

sincerity. In his work as a whole, in his manner of creating, he remained essentially an anarchist. This is why classical compositions appear side by side with compositions in shorthand, and at the same time austere works of Cubist inspiration are followed by monsters of an unleashed fantasy. His courage, which made him prefer sincerity to perfection, gave him a previously unknown freedom.

But it would be erroneous to see in Picasso the haughtily aloof artist, who created only for the sake of recording his own sensations, who produced merely a painted autobiography. He was always able to transcend the small domain of his personal adventures; from the outset he raised them to the universally human level. This is why he created his hallucinating monsters and at the same time the classical figures which he saw with an affectionate eye. He never hesitated to give to classical idealization its counterpart of whimsical and ugly demonism. Aside from being a great creator of forms and language, he was a powerful creator of myths, of beauty, and ugliness, of life in everything. Because he truly committed himself to the current of life, his art succeeds in encompassing this life in its totality. This fact earned him the reputation of a split personality, an errant soul. He was an errant soul, but only in the sense of his fellow countryman, Don Quixote, the Knight Errant, who preferred adventure to barren security. He devoted himself to the adventure of authenticity, and thanks to his prodigious, magical imagination, he succeeded in turning his adventures into plastic signs. His life's work, whose richness is not confined by any preconceived system, presents a surprising, unexpected variety; it revealed to his contemporaries a new conception of man, man who refuses to become slave to any system, even his own, but rather who dedicates himself to life with all its ups and downs, its hopes and disappointments, and hence to sincerity, to absolute authenticity. It is through this authenticity that Picasso exemplifies the *amor fati* about which Nietzsche wrote; it is through his love of life, which he lived so intensely, that he has been, during the more than seventy years of his artistic career, and in the sum total of his immense painted, sculptured, and graphic work, a guide to his contemporaries and to our century.

DRAWINGS AND PRINTS

GRAPHIC TECHNIQUES were important to Picasso: to his paintings, ceramics, and sculptures we must add his drawings, etchings, lithographs, linoleum cuts, and related works. They reveal just how many octaves and registers the artist had at his disposal, with which to build up the astonishing polyphony of his life's work.

It is especially typical of Picasso's graphic style, no doubt, that his drawings constitute a voice of their own within his work as a whole. The drawings are not just preliminary studies, mere preludes to works executed in other mediums. On the contrary, Picasso's drawings are quite independent of his other works, and in many periods of his rich creative career—above all, when he was sacrificing color to his concentration on form—we find him most inventive in his drawings. He does not apply his new discoveries to paintings, at least not right away: for instance, the realistic drawings of 1915 precede by three years the paintings in a similar style. And he continued to develop the flexible, clear linear style of his "Ingres period" for years in drawings and prints, although he abandoned it in painting around 1925. Many more such examples could be cited.

Thus, Picasso's graphic works—prints as well as drawings—form an entirely autonomous domain within the broad panorama of his oeuvre. And it is proper to observe that within this domain we find the same richness and diversity as in the other domains of Picasso's art. This is not only true of techniques, but also of conceptions. Technically, the artist made himself master of all the graphic methods, in addition to drawing—etching (which he practiced at an early date), lithography, and linoleum cuts (a fairly late development). At the same time, he mastered the whole range of rich expressive means—from the most austere stiff-pen drawings to dynamic, painterly brush drawings. For this reason we must not be surprised that his drawings quite often go beyond the bounds that set them off from painting: we must not underestimate the part played by drawing in the collages of 1913. The richness of Picasso's graphic work comes not only from the variety of techniques and expressive means, but above all from the use Picasso made of these techniques and means. Each technique provided him with a new method for discovering things hitherto unrealized, merely latent, in another technique. Picasso's "playing with" the various techniques was a process of experimentation that stopped only when he had exhausted the potentialities of a new medium. Thus his production of graphic works tended to be bunched at particular periods of his life and creative career. For instance, the rich and varied series of lithographs executed in Mourlot's workshop date from the period between 1945 and the spring of 1949: before, Picasso had not exhibited great interest in the medium.

Besides the drawings and engravings proper, there are Picasso's book illustrations. Except for one etching of 1905, he did not attempt this type of work until 1911, when he illustrated Max Jacob's *Saint Matorel*. He never wholly abandoned it thereafter. What strikes us in this field is the richness, not only of technical execution, but still more of artistic conception.

A characteristic feature of Picasso's graphic works is that many fall into a cycle or series—the series *The Painter and His Model*, for instance, and *Bullfights*. In such sequences, an underlying theme is varied in most surprising ways, ever with fresh invention. One of the finest examples of how these variations on a theme lead to the discovery of new creative solutions is the group of drawings for *Guernica* (a few of which are shown in figures 29–33) and the series of such prints as *The Dream and Lie of Franco,* which preceded them. Here we see that Picasso, far from looking upon drawings as purely prelimi-nary studies, never carried over into painting the literal results of his graphic researches. Rather, drawing and engraving had for him the same creative dignity that he acknowledged in the other domains of his art.

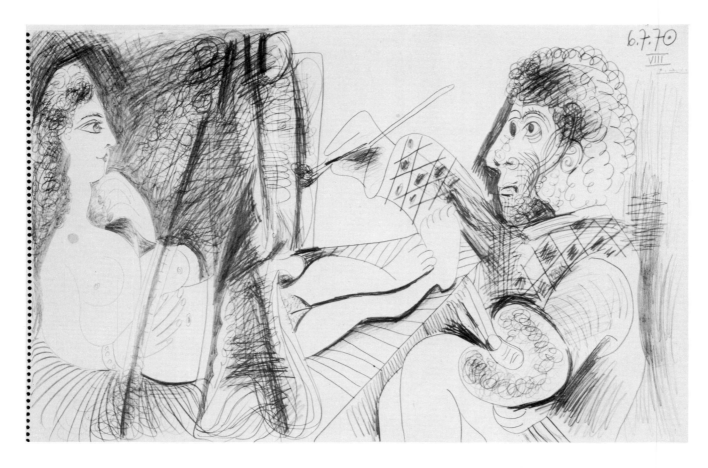

64. THE PAINTER AND HIS MODEL. 1970. Crayon, 12^1/$_4$ × 19^1/$_4$''.
Galerie Louise Leiris, Paris

COLORPLATES

Painted 1901

CHILD WITH A DOVE

Oil on canvas, 28³/₄ × 21¹/₄″

Anonymous Loan to the National Gallery, London

This is one of Picasso's earliest works: he was twenty-one, or even less, but his own style is already apparent. He probably painted it in Paris during his second visit, when he was staying with Spanish friends. By that time he had seen, studied, and assimilated contemporary French painting: he had taken Toulouse-Lautrec's way of rendering a visual impression rapidly with a few forceful lines and shrill spots of color, and made it his own. Also, he had learned from Degas how to observe a figure sharply and with detachment. In *Child with a Dove*, we see a new thoughtfulness, a poetic sympathy with the subject, qualities that were to dominate his work in the years that followed.

The masters who served as Picasso's mentors in the early years of his career —Toulouse-Lautrec and Degas—had observed and set down the figures they painted with cool objectivity. Picasso had followed their example in his earliest works; but here, a new relationship is introduced between the figure observed and the observer: a relationship of empathy, of human sympathy. And in this early work we find a feature of Picasso's painting that was to characterize his subsequent work: the painter is deeply involved, wholeheartedly caught up in the object represented.

Possibly the reason for so intimate an approach to the subject lies in the subject of this particular work. Picasso's father, Don José Ruiz, had made pigeons a particularly favored subject of his paintings, and as a boy Picasso must often have seen pigeons, as well as his father's pictures of them. Childhood memories must surely have been involved.

The pictorial technique, however, is quite new, and it too is interesting for all that was to happen later. The forms are rendered in simple sweeping lines, and the colors are keyed to an untroubled three-tone scale in which greenish tones dominate. The shimmering Impressionist palette which Picasso had brought to Paris, and which he had used up to now, is here discarded. The colors are subdued, controlled by an austere swoop of line.

This painting comes well before Picasso's Blue Period—and it is perhaps the earliest of his works in which he appears as a clearly defined individuality. He seems to have left his apprenticeship behind, giving us for the first time an expression of his own, not very gay vision of the world. It was a vision he shared with others of his generation at the turn of the century, to whom the world they saw around them seemed a paradise lost.

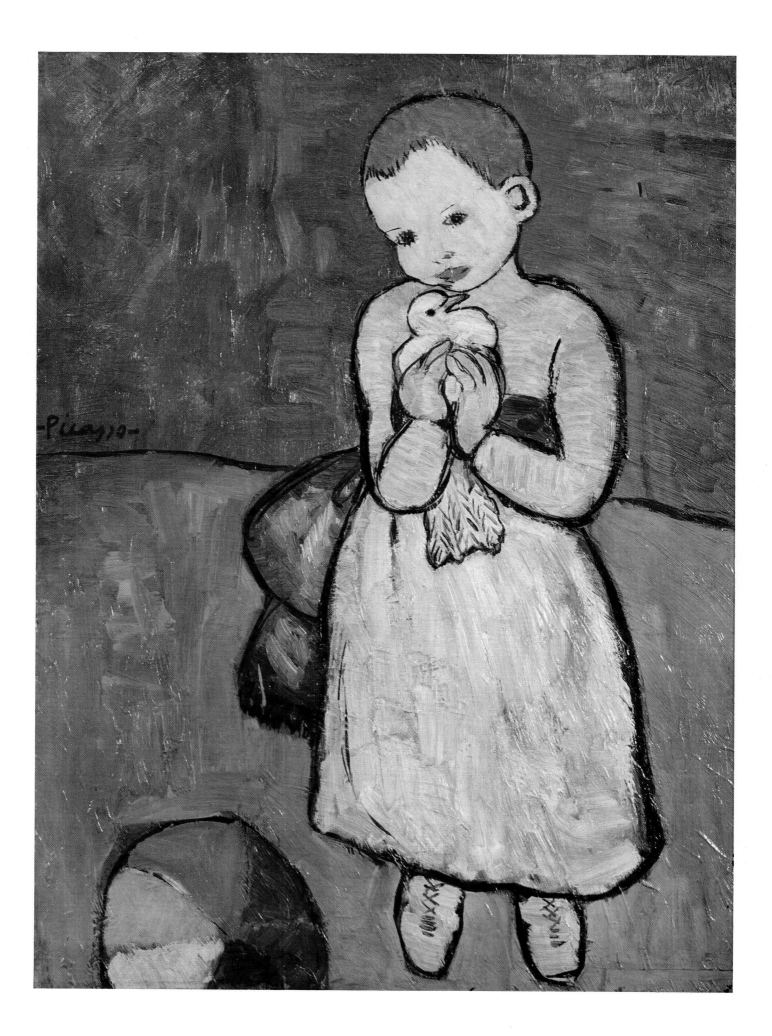

Painted 1903

LA VIE

Oil on canvas, $77^3/8 \times 50^5/8''$
The Cleveland Museum of Art (Gift of the Hanna Fund)

This allegorical painting is the largest single work Picasso produced in his Blue
Period, so-called from the melancholy cold blue tones that dominate his work
during the years 1901–1904. His paintings throughout this period express social
pessimism, dejection, and despair, almost unrelievedly. The subjects are mostly
the destitute—beggars, blind men, street musicians, lost women. The portray-
al of their misery is further accentuated by the spare austerity of the drawing,
and by a palette restricted to the gloomiest, coldest colors.

La Vie is an allegorical summing-up of the artist's vision of life in those years.
For all its pictorial and symbolic qualities, it remains, as Alfred H. Barr, Jr.,
has said, "a problematical" work. It challenges interpretation, but the emotional content comes through unmistakably. Two nude figures—a man and a
young woman—stand at the left, facing a clothed female at the right edge of
the canvas, who holds a little child in the folds of her cape. Between them two
sketches hang above one another on the back wall of the room. The top one
shows a nude couple huddled together in gloomy dejection; the lower one
represents a nude female figure crouching listlessly on the ground, her head on
her knees. The picture as a whole is deeply disturbing.

There are unmistakable autobiographical references in this painting. Preliminary sketches show beyond a doubt that the male figure is a self-portrait
of the artist. Yet somehow the artist is already transcending his personal fate,
creating a work of universal significance.

In its thematic material, the work is akin to similar allegorizations of daily
life which the Jugendstil (Art Nouveau) had made fashionable. What Picasso
has in common with these other artists is a pessimistic outlook, expressed not
only in the symbolism of the figures. but also—primarily—in the desolate blues
of the painting. It is a sense of the hopelessness of life, which is socially determined—something like what Rilke expressed in his poems in the same years.
What makes the canvas so unequivocally Picasso's is the terseness with which
he has said what he has to say. All the works of his Blue Period raise the features
of human misery and social despair to classical terms. The austerity of the
figures is perfectly matched in the color quality of the palette.

As we have said, *La Vie* is the most important work of these years. Although
interpretations of given details may vary, it is certain that this allegory evokes
life as it must have been or seemed at the beginning of our century, and this
Picasso expressed magnificently in the works of his Blue Period.

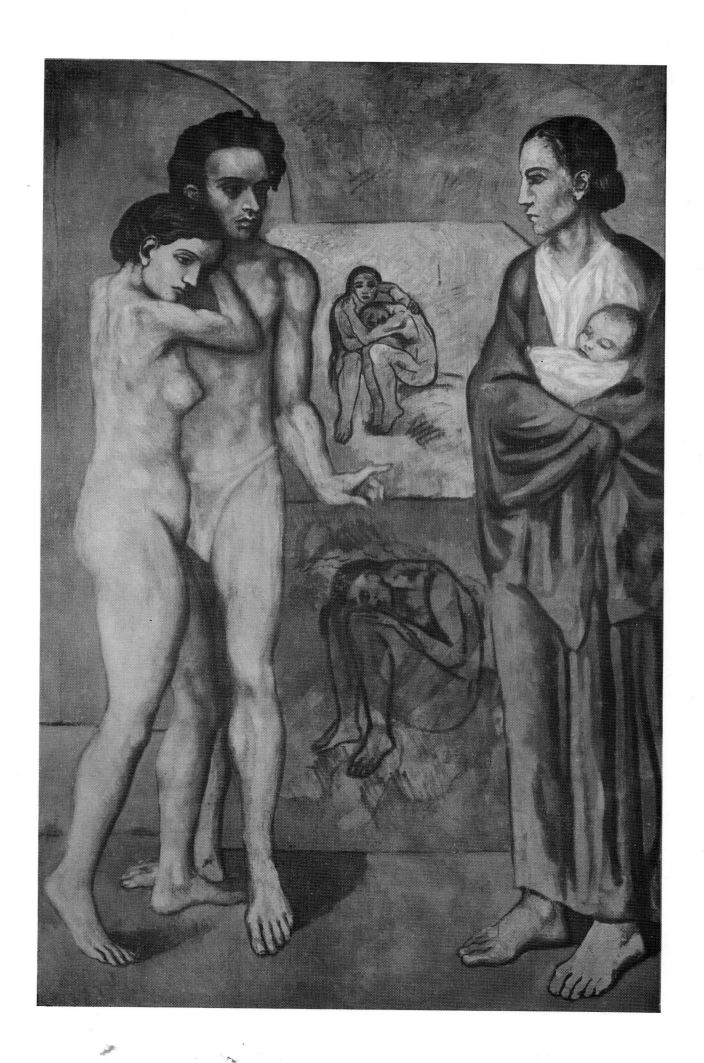

Painted 1904

LA REPASSEUSE (WOMAN IRONING)

Oil on canvas, 45³/₄ × 28³/₄″

The Solomon R. Guggenheim Museum, New York (The Justin K. Thannhauser Collection)

In this work a single figure conveys the misery and tragedy which Picasso treated more allegorically in the big canvas *La Vie*. The originality of *La Repasseuse* becomes clearer when we compare it with Degas' treatment of the same subject, in a different spirit (figure 7).

In Degas' painting a woman is caught yawning and stretching after a long day's ironing. The picture's astonishing power comes primarily from the unconventional boldness of observation, but this keeps it within the realm of genre painting. Picasso's work, on the other hand, is as far from a genre scene as one can get. The figure rises above her sphere of everyday life like a saint's image. She symbolizes all the women like her who have labored for ages. The artist has gone far beyond mere observation, immediate perception. He has distilled the very emblem of a workaday life, transcending its accidental character, expressing its essence.

The austere, hieratic quality of this painting shows an influence of El Greco: the elongated limbs and the stark silhouette go back to the great Spanish painter whom Picasso admired very early. Here some of El Greco's stylistic devices are turned to use in a contemporary subject, the servitude of modern labor. Picasso sees the woman ironing as "a revered martyr of human society," no less sublime than El Greco's saints and martyrs.

The austerity and spareness of the forms and colors in this painting are admirably in tune with the subject; defined in a few lines, the figure is set against a simple background distinguished only by its coloring. This spareness of means characterizes much of Picasso's art in the early years of the century. Scornful of easy effects, the artist realizes his deeper intentions, to portray human misery not just in its tragic implications, but also in its ennobling power. Picasso's figure becomes a symbol of humanity spiritualized, enduring the servitude of labor with resignation but also with dignity. Picasso's image of man in these years reflects an attitude that was not unusual at the beginning of the century— assigning greater weight to spiritual values than to the observation of visible reality. In his works of the Blue Period, Picasso was paving the way for a wholly spiritual kind of painting, no longer limited by contingencies of perception.

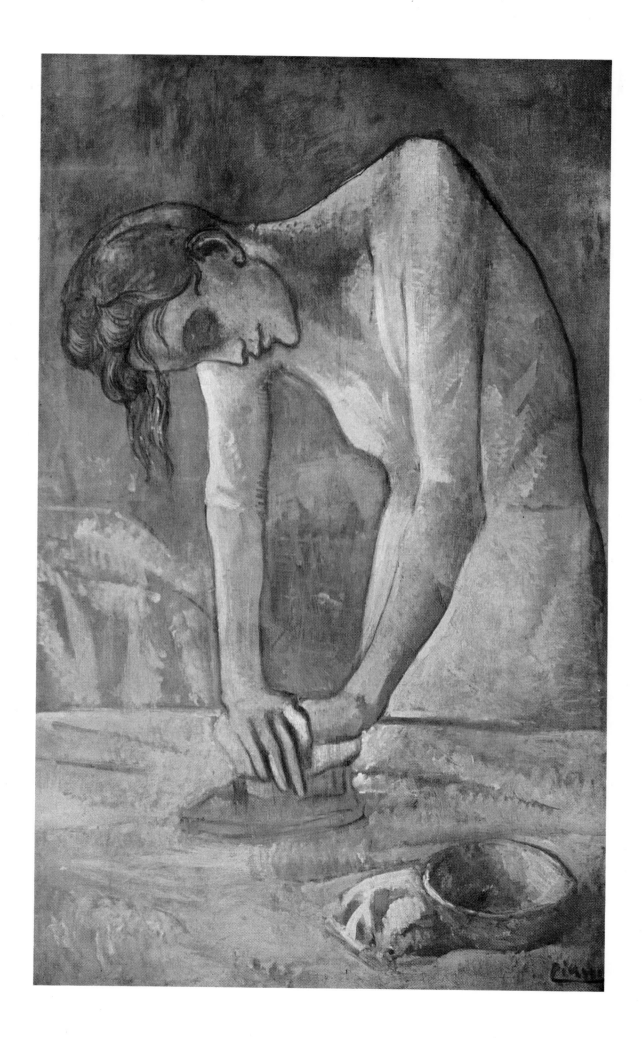

Painted 1905

AT THE LAPIN AGILE
(ARLEQUIN AU VERRE)

Oil on canvas, 39 × 39¹/₂″

The Estate of Joan W. Payson

This painting, sometimes entitled *Harlequin with Glass,* dates from the same time as *La Repasseuse.* During this year Picasso's style underwent changes determined in part by personal reasons, yet at the same time reflecting rapid maturation of talent.

Leaving behind the joyless world of the Blue Period—of which *La Repasseuse* is a striking example—Picasso now arrived at the new colors that characterize *At the Lapin Agile.* He is no longer so pessimistic about life; for the first time he begins to celebrate it.

This is one of several paintings in which Picasso documented the life of the performers in circus and carnival which he frequented from time to time while he was living in the so-called Bateau-lavoir in Montmartre. But this painting is more than a discovery of new subject matter. Picasso portrays himself in the figure of Harlequin, identifying himself with his "fellow performers," and with their melancholy, their sense of loneliness. Yet we do not seem quite so hopelessly cut off from the rest of the world here as in the paintings of the Blue Period. There are people clustering around Harlequin, for all that he is on the margin of society, as all artists were in the early part of the century.

We feel that Picasso has come up a bit in the world—living with congenial fellow artists in Montmartre, and having met Fernande Olivier. Besides, the picture shows growing artistic maturity. The shrill colors which characterized Picasso's earliest works in Paris have gone, and with them his indebtedness to such models as Steinlen and Toulouse-Lautrec. The strong reds, yellows, and greens are clearly set off from the warm brownish background; the figures, flat and distinctly articulated, in turn articulate the space. This space is no longer the blank, uninhabitable space of the Blue Period, but a space that is felt— though barely indicated—in which people are yet together, related to each other, if only by listening to the same guitar.

With the first paintings from this new period in Picasso's development, to which this work certainly belongs, Picasso takes mastery of a whole world of his own. No longer obsessed with those purely conceptual figures which abounded in the Blue Period, he now begins to grope timidly for contact with his fellow men. Harlequin's effort to get closer to the world around him, for all his enormous vulnerability, is so sympathetic, so human, that he becomes a compelling symbol. As always in Picasso's art, even in this early work technique and subject are combined in a meaningful whole.

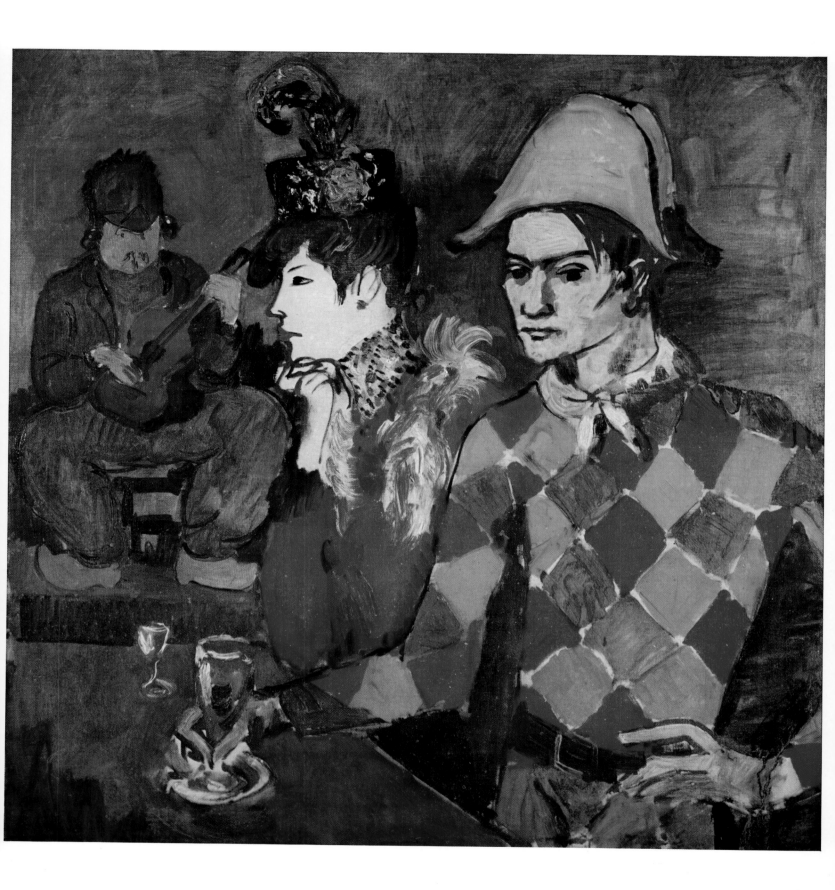

Painted 1905

FAMILY OF SALTIMBANQUES

Oil on canvas, $83^3/4 \times 90^3/8''$

National Gallery of Art, Washington, D.C. (Chester Dale Collection)

This large composition required a long period of preparation. It was Picasso's main work of 1905, and marks a transition to his Rose Period. The gloomy images of human misery have given way to paintings in which pale rose is the dominant tonality, and the life of circus performers is the theme. Picasso at this time lived not very far from the Paris circus, and it deeply impressed him. The segregation, the loneliness, the gentleness of these people disclosed new aspects of human society to him.

Picasso's paintings of 1905 turn away from social pessimism—their dominant color suggests a lyrical, personal sadness rather than pessimistic despair. The figures exhibit a certain life in common, though the psychological relationships are not clear. As it was in *La Vie* (page 51), the unity of the composition lies in the emotional content more than in the legible details. The over-all sense of restraint is more striking here than in the earlier work: it is accentuated by the fact that the two figures closest to the viewer are seen from the back. The colors, which range from terracotta pink and ocher to gray and bright blue, suggest the same restraint. The color effects are everywhere subdued, reduced to a discreet, unobtrusive harmony. The drawing and the colors endow this painting with a quiet, oddly elegiac charm.

The mood of this work inspired the opening lines of Rainer Maria Rilke's fifth Duino Elegy:

But tell me, who are they, these travellers, even a little | more fleeting than we ourselves,— so urgently, ever since childhood | wrung by an (oh, for the sake of whom?) | never-contented will? That keeps on wringing them, bending them, slinging them, swinging them, | throwing them and catching them back: as though from an oily, | smoother air, they come down on the threadbare carpet, thinned by their everlasting | upspringing, this carpet forlornly | lost in the cosmos. | Laid on like a plaster, as though the suburban sky | had injured the earth there.*

Although this work reveals the artist's new sense of kinship with his environment, it continues the meditative mood of the previous years. Here, as in the earlier works, the figures are not unified as a group by the performance of some common action; any similarity to a genre scene is excluded by the spirituality of the figures, expressing melancholy tenderness rather than resigned despair. This tenderness is clearly conveyed—precisely because the colors are subdued—by the flowing lines, so very different from the harsh, angular lines of the preceding period. Now Picasso becomes increasingly interested in drawing; we have a few etchings from these same years, and his first sculpture, *Head of a Harlequin*, also dates from this time (figure 9). Concentration on the possibilities of line ushers in a new period in Picasso's art, one in striking contrast to his Fauve and earliest Expressionist works, in which color predominated over line.

* Rainer Maria Rilke, *The Duino Elegies,* translated by J. B. Leishman and Stephen Spender. The Hogarth Press, London, 1963 (4th edition, revised).

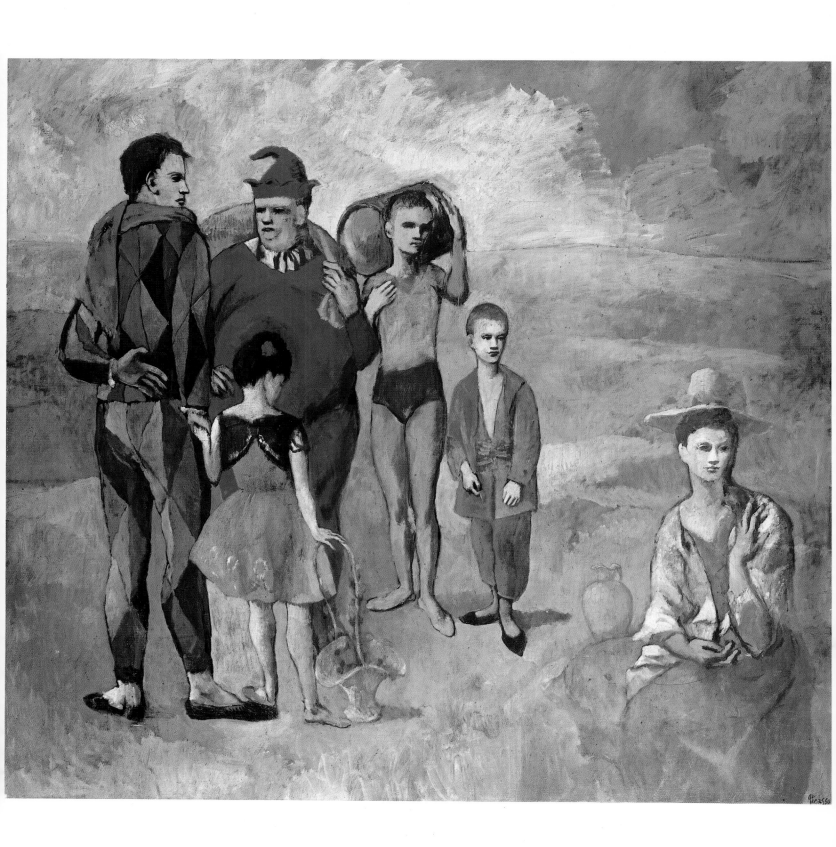

Painted 1906

LA COIFFURE

Oil on canvas, 68⁷/₈ × 39¹/₄″

The Metropolitan Museum of Art, New York (Purchase, Anonymous gift)

In 1906 Picasso's style discloses a new development which, however, arises naturally enough out of his work in the years just preceding. Composition or structure take on greater importance, and produce an almost classical restraint and unity.

La Coiffure is one of the finest works of this period, outstanding in its classical calm and objectivity. The three figures form a pyramid, in keeping with the concept of figure composition which had been current in classical painting since Leonardo. This rigorously ordered work may have been inspired by Picasso's study of classical painting in The Louvre. The young artist may also have been influenced by the art of Cézanne, represented at the Salon d'Automne in 1905 by ten important paintings in which compositional values are deliberately emphasized. Even earlier, while still a student in Spain, Picasso had been greatly drawn to the classical current in French painting, and admired its leading living representative, Puvis de Chavannes.

It is to the classical spirit of such masters that Picasso's work in the second half of 1906 comes close. Among these works *La Coiffure* stands out most prominently. The calm and balance of the composition overshadows psychological and lyrical elements: the figures are subordinated to the part they play in the compositional arrangement. Moreover—perhaps for the first time in Picasso's career—the composition takes account of spatial values. The pyramidal pattern and the volumes of the bodies suggest depth to a degree never seen before in Picasso's paintings: the artist had made little attempt to represent it before. Now, having made his first sculptures—the *Head of a Harlequin* dates from this same time (figure 9)—Picasso is more aware of the potentialities of plastic effects, and these contribute to the unity and dignity of his paintings in the classical manner.

In the first years of the century Picasso's development led him from sympathy for the wretched plight of his subjects to a less troubled spirit of acceptance, a feeling that he shared their fate. The virile maturity of paintings like *La Coiffure* is very different from the youthful sentimentality expressed in some earlier works. It is remarkable that Picasso achieved such maturity so early—before his twenty-fifth birthday. At the same time, for all their clearly marked individuality, these works are a preparation for the works of the subsequent years—works in which he will achieve mastery of the means of traditional painting, so as to be able to turn his back on it and launch his journey of discovery into hitherto unknown domains of painting. *La Coiffure* marks the point where mastery was finally reached, and will soon be left behind.

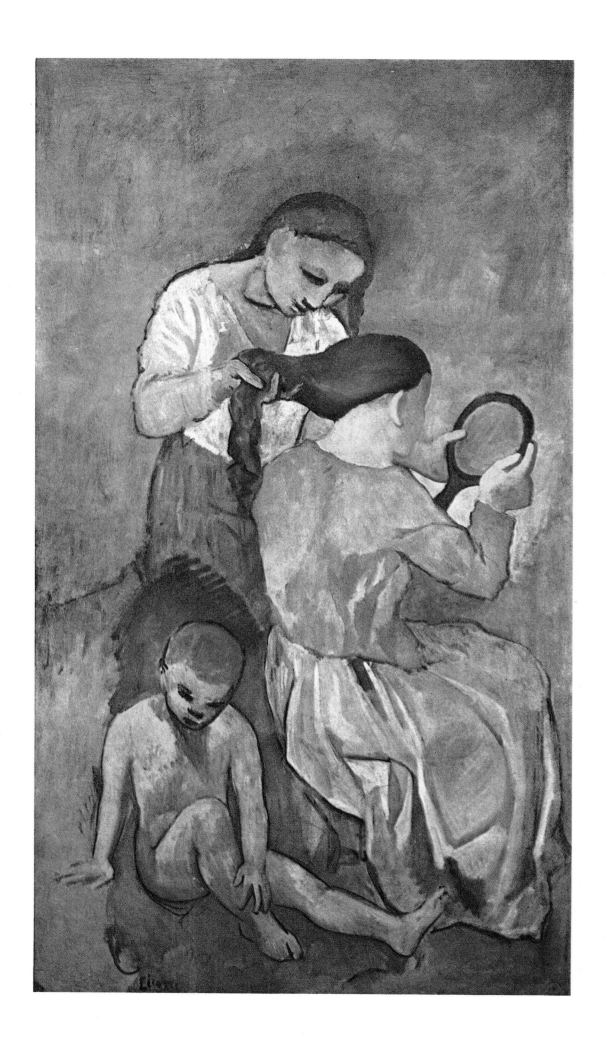

Painted 1906

GERTRUDE STEIN

Oil on canvas, 39¹/₄ × 32"

The Metropolitan Museum of Art, New York (Gertrude Stein Bequest)

This work ushers in a new phase in Picasso's art. It also represents a gesture of friendly gratitude to one of his earliest patrons and purchasers, a tribute to Miss Stein's imposing personality. Gertrude Stein and her brother Leo belonged to the first generation of Americans who took an active part in the twentieth century's artistic revolutions in Europe—especially in Paris. The Steins' house in Paris became a meeting place for European and American intellectuals. As early as 1905 the Steins bought a painting by Picasso; they had already demonstrated their open-mindedness to new departures in art by buying a Matisse. It was at their house that Picasso met Matisse, a meeting that was the beginning of a long friendship between the two masters which ended only with Matisse's death in 1953.

Picasso began this portrait of Gertrude Stein in the spring of 1906. He asked her to sit for him, and she tells us herself how long he worked at it—there were at least eighty sittings—and how far from satisfied he was at every stage. It is characteristic of his conception of art—this applies generally to all the new painting at that time—that in the course of this experience he reached the conviction that the presence of the sitter was really unnecessary.

Toward the end of spring Picasso stopped working on the portrait and took a trip to Gosol in northern Spain. There his style began to change: perhaps he was influenced by the stark, treeless mountain surroundings. Alone and hard at work, Picasso turned away from the classical balanced treatment he had evolved, and let himself be inspired by primitive, archaic forms. The plasticity of the bodies had been becoming pronounced in the works done immediately before, and it now took on further emphasis: he abandoned the meticulous treatment of details for a broader, synthetic conception of form. As has been justly observed, Picasso was encouraged in his new tendency by the early Iberian sculptures exhibited for the first time at The Louvre in 1906.

Back in Paris at the end of the summer, Picasso resumed work on this portrait. Without seeing his sitter again he painted the face—nearly all the rest had been completed before. It is in the face, whose masklike starkness contrasts so sharply with the treatment of the rest of the portrait, that we see the new development in Picasso's style. Instead of reproducing visible appearances, he is now moving toward the magical re-creation of reality. To those who criticized this portrait, Picasso replied: "Nobody thinks it is a good likeness, but never mind, in the end she is going to look just like that." For the first time in Picasso's art, the artist's vision has triumphed over sense perception.

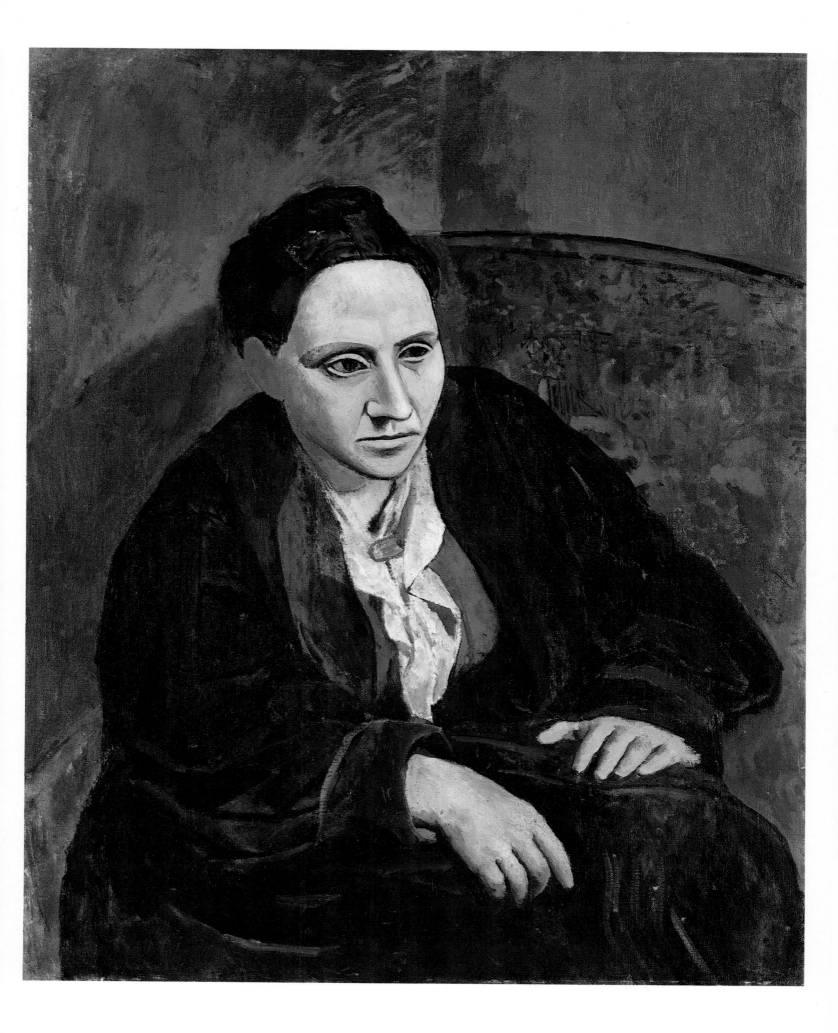

Painted 1906

SELF-PORTRAIT

Oil on canvas, 36¹/₄ × 28³/₄″
Philadelphia Museum of Art (A. E. Gallatin Collection)

Picasso incorporated his own features in a number of early works, though seldom in the form of explicit self-portraits. Aside from the self-portrait in the National Gallery in Prague (figure 12), which dates from 1907, the one shown here is the last he ever painted. It is hard to say why, but one reason is surely the fact that around 1906 Picasso lost interest in human psychology and turned all his attention to problems of form.

Thus, the self-portrait of 1906 stands between two periods of Picasso's art: it heralds a new style aiming at spatial values. A clear indication of this new tendency is the fact that in this painting he almost entirely renounces color, restricting it largely to the triad of gray, white, and ocher. Only the palette that Picasso holds in his left hand shows a bit of red and a darker ocher tone.

Precisely because of this near-absence of color, the forms in space and the volumes of the body are brought out the more strongly. The figure of the artist is projected into space and creates its own field of spatial energy by the impact of its three-dimensionality. As a result, the fact that Picasso did not achieve this effect through modeling but through the suggestion of a few sharp outlines, is all the more striking. Nor is there any question of light effects in this all-but-colorless portrait: Picasso is aiming at the essential characteristics of the surfaces, trying to paraphrase them in the same way as the plastic values. The gripping effect of the portrait rests primarily on its spatial structure.

Here the twenty-five-year-old Picasso displays complete mastery of his means. At the same time, we catch a hint that he is no longer satisfied with these means, that he is groping toward new ones in view of attaining another goal. The revolution in painting that he was to touch off in the next few years is already anticipated in this work. All attempts at psychological treatment of the human figure have been abandoned, and the artist is no longer primarily aiming at producing a likeness. The painting has a supra-personal order, a firmly-knit structure in its own right. It is noteworthy that this same year Picasso produced a sculpture—a bronze head—which realizes the same idea of form, and also anticipates future developments (figure 15).

The figure that confronts the viewer in this work is more than just a portrait of the young artist: it is a work in which Picasso sums up his achievements to date and readies himself for the fresh start that will lead him ever farther afield—the exploration of a new world of space, volume, and order.

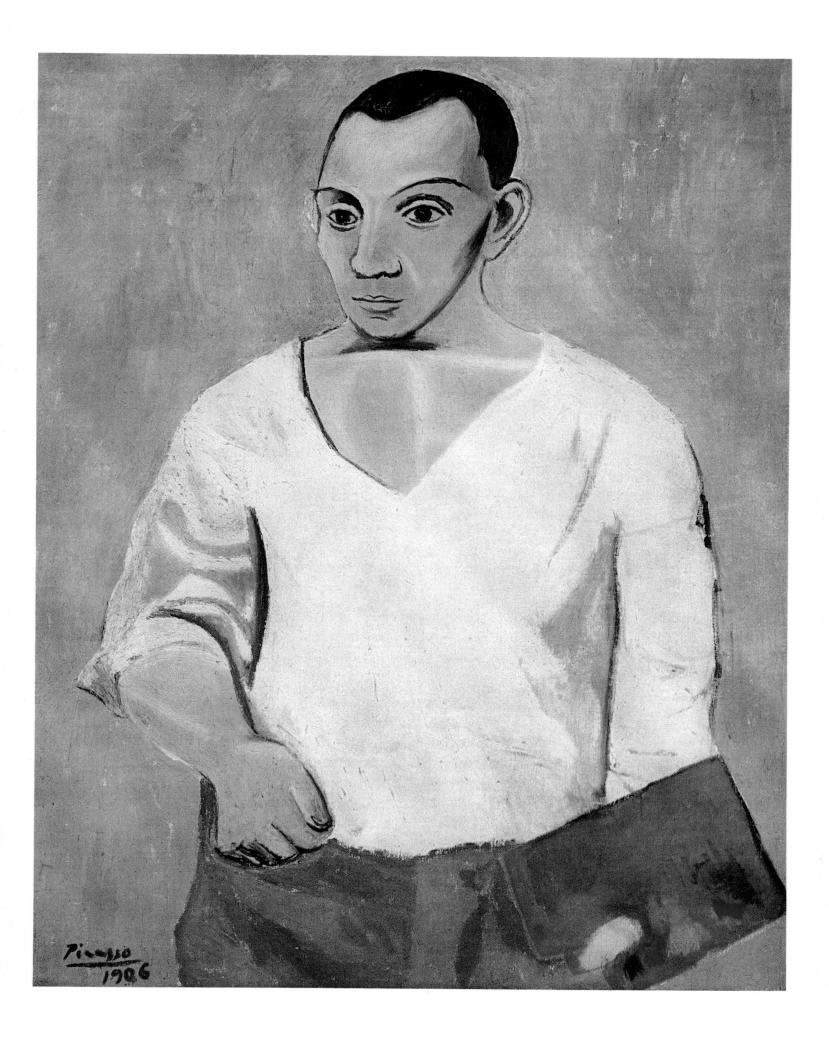

Painted 1907

LES DEMOISELLES D'AVIGNON

Oil on canvas, 96 × 92"

The Museum of Modern Art, New York (Lillie P. Bliss Bequest)

This large enigmatic canvas marks a turning point, and not merely in Picasso's development. It is more than a painting, it is a revolutionary breakthrough in the history of modern art. Picasso worked a very long time on it, making many sketches, and it reflects the struggle of the artist in arriving at a new style. While the central figures still bear witness to the stage when the painting was first conceived, the nudes that frame the composition disclose an entirely new, revolutionary step forward.

The painting shows a figurative composition of five nudes grouped around a still life in the foreground. In structure, it harks back to Cézanne's figurative works, in which nudes are arranged as an architecture of bodies. The title of the painting—it was probably named by André Salmon some time after it had been completed—suggests some brothel scene. The earliest preliminary sketches, however, suggest that originally the artist intended an allegory of transitory life, a subject similar to that of *La Vie*, painted in 1903 (page 51). But as Picasso went on working, the anecdotal and allegorical details were eliminated one by one, and in its final stage the painting owes its overwhelming effect not to any eloquence of literary association, but to the compelling force of the pictorial idiom.

Just what has happened? In this great composition Picasso follows up the new line of development which had started with Cézanne's rigorous nude compositions, but extends still further back to primitive humanity's earliest, most rudimentary experiments with form. All the secondary elements, including all allegorical associations, were gradually sloughed off as the painter kept working on this picture. The large forms of the bodies confront the viewer in all their angular, grandiosely conceived ponderousness. How the new style evolved can be traced in the picture itself: the central figures disclose the simplified structure of the paintings done the year before, and in their masklike repose the heads are reminiscent of the portrait of Gertrude Stein; but the figures at either side, especially their heads, disclose a new treatment. They have been built up out of large, firmly defined planes, which are no longer modeled by light and by the contours that light reveals, but are as though hacked out with knife and chisel. Especially do the heads of the two nudes at the right reveal the will to new form: the most dramatic contrasts supplant ordinary transitions, and thus in magic violence the new pictorial idiom is born. Even the space in which the figures stand seems to be sculptured—it is not an atmosphere, as in the earlier works, but a volume, a mass. It is still an open question whether Picasso was aided in this crucial advance by examples of African Negro sculpture, which was just being discovered in these years. At all events, he achieved here a style which raises the sculptural structure of the work to magical significance. With this exploit he pointed the way to the Cubist revolution.

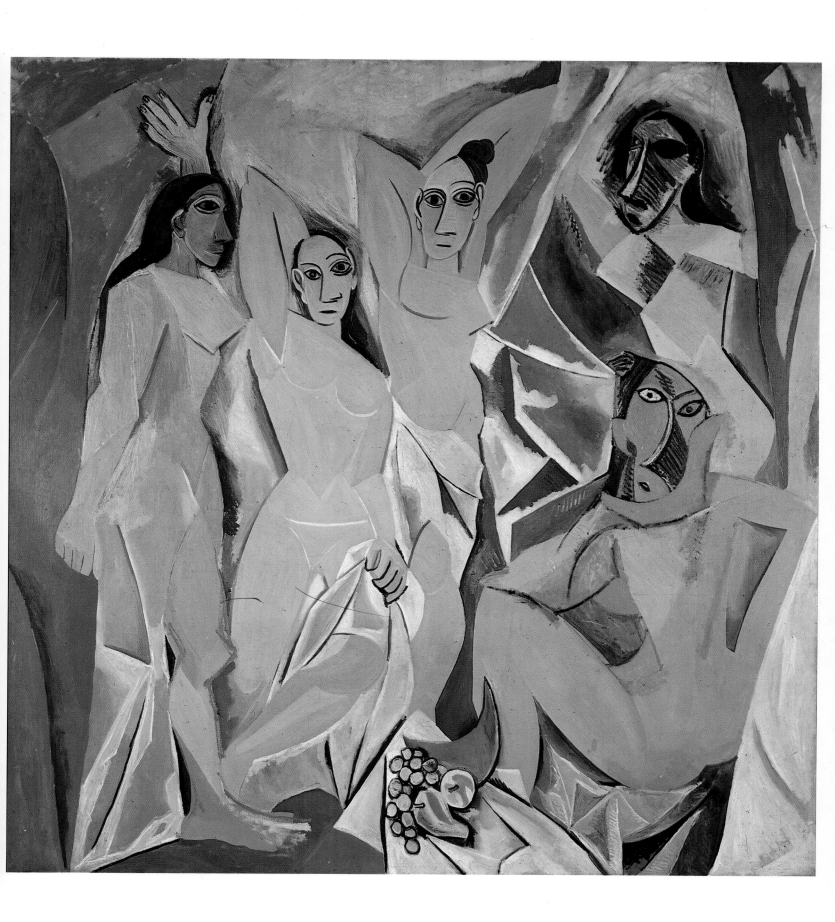

Painted 1908

DRYAD

Oil on canvas, $72^7/8 \times 42^1/2''$
The Hermitage, Leningrad

This figure, a nude among trees, marks a further advance in the direction Picasso had been taking ever since *Les Demoiselles d'Avignon*. He painted it in the summer of 1908 while staying at La Rue-des-Bois on the Oise, near Paris. The work is redolent of carefree holidays.

For the first time in Picasso's new phase, landscape—man's natural environment—plays a part in the composition: trees and other greenery surround the central figure. The world of plants and trees, hitherto almost wholly absent from Picasso's painting, is treated in the same way as the human figure: the foliage becomes compact masses, and, like the figure, the over-all effect is sculptural. And so Picasso achieves a new kind of synthesis between man and nature—in contrast with Impressionist art, in which trees, plants, and the human figure tended to be dissolved in a shimmer of atmospheric color. Now, in Picasso's newer works, a new conception of landscape is making itself felt: the things of nature become solid and tangible, fill up the pictorial space, and in their spatial aspects are treated as equals of the human figure.

Not only trees, plants, and the forms of nature have become more solid; space itself has become solid and tangible. The painter treats it in the same sculptural manner as the human figure and the natural forms. As a result the painting becomes a firm architectonic unit. Picasso builds up his painting with pieces of space, with the figure, and with the forms of nature. Even the stones are made to obey the same law.

Yet Picasso's paintings during these months, for all the rigidity of their structure, clearly reflect the rest and relaxation of a stay in the country. Color— the color of the Ile de France, the saturated, luscious green—once again appears in these works. To be sure, Picasso's palette is extremely restricted: just as he renounces transitions between forms, and builds compositions out of the simplest formal elements, so he imposes strict limits on color: he confines himself to brown, ocher, and green. They clarify the formal structure, while conceding precedence to form. Nevertheless, it is the color in these works that gives them a freer, broader sense of life. Having lingered in a world primarily determined by the human figure, Picasso has come out of doors at last. Physical rest and relaxation seem to be at work in this development, which led the artist to magnificent paintings that give the synthesis between man and nature this new universal form.

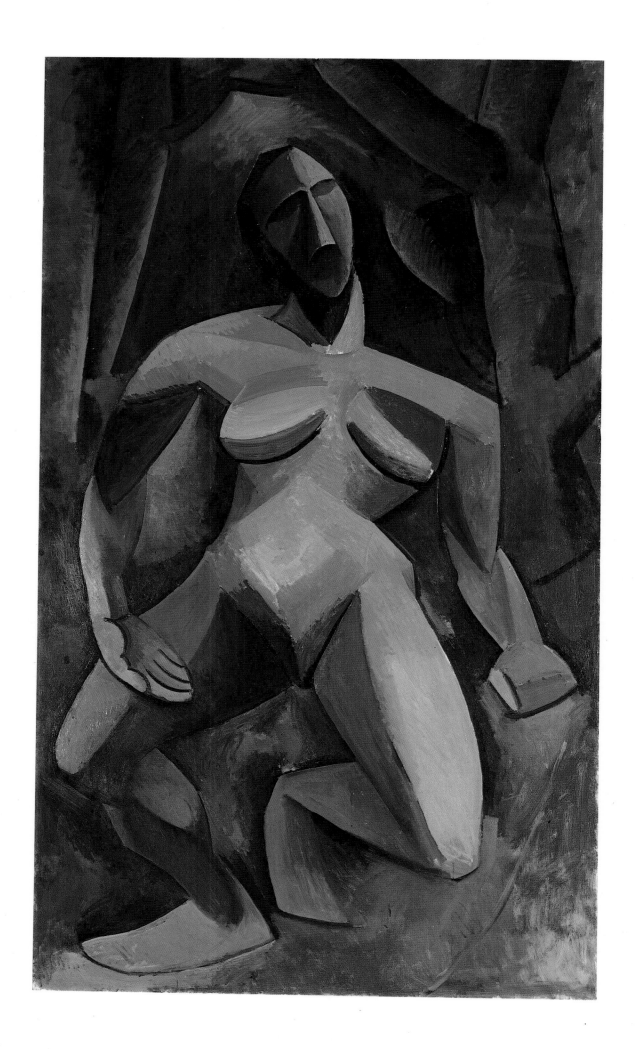

Painted 1909

THE RESERVOIR AT HORTA DE EBRO

Oil on canvas, 23³/4 × 19³/4″
Private collection, New York

The pictorial conquest of nature that began in 1908 reached its high point the following year. Picasso spent the summer at Horta de Ebro, and the austere bare forms of the local landscape inspired a number of magnificent paintings; the one shown here is perhaps the best.

This work is distinguished from the works of the preceding years, above all, by the ruthless logic of its composition. Whereas in 1907 and 1908 Picasso was primarily inspired by the massive compactness of primitive sculpture, his idea-pattern has here become the crystal, that most geometric of all nature's formations. Cézanne's tremendous attempt to reduce natural form to the simplest geometric bodies and thus to create "a harmony parallel to nature" was probably what set Picasso on the road to this new conception of nature. The landscapes painted by his friend Braque at L'Estaque, near Marseilles, in 1908 may have been a still more immediate stimulus to Picasso, who here applies his newly acquired grammar of vision to landscape. It was these landscapes by Braque—and probably also those by Picasso—which led contemporary art critics, sometimes jeeringly yet not inaptly, to coin the term "Cubist."

The rigor with which the parts of the picture are joined together to form a regular whole at once suggests the structure of a crystal. Color plays a subordinate role, being confined to a few shades of yellow, ocher, and green; form wholly predominates. Obeying the laws of a clear, spiritualized syntax, the forms constitute a unity which is no longer derived from sense perception but is governed by the inner law of the painting, by its own pictorial language. As in a fugue, the individual themes overlap and follow one another; the predominantly mathematical basis, too, relates these paintings to the fugue in music. Their effect is just as classical and austere, and rests entirely upon the rigorous application of a clear, intellectually rigorous principle of composition.

The self-sufficiency of this painting is further stressed by the fact that color and light no longer serve to render the visible forms of the object, but solely to strengthen the unity and architectonic structure of the work as a whole. In paintings such as this one, Picasso shows what inflexible self-discipline is required to create a new pictorial language. With these landscapes he also took another step away from dependence upon the object, and toward the autonomous work of art, conceived of as a harmony parallel to nature.

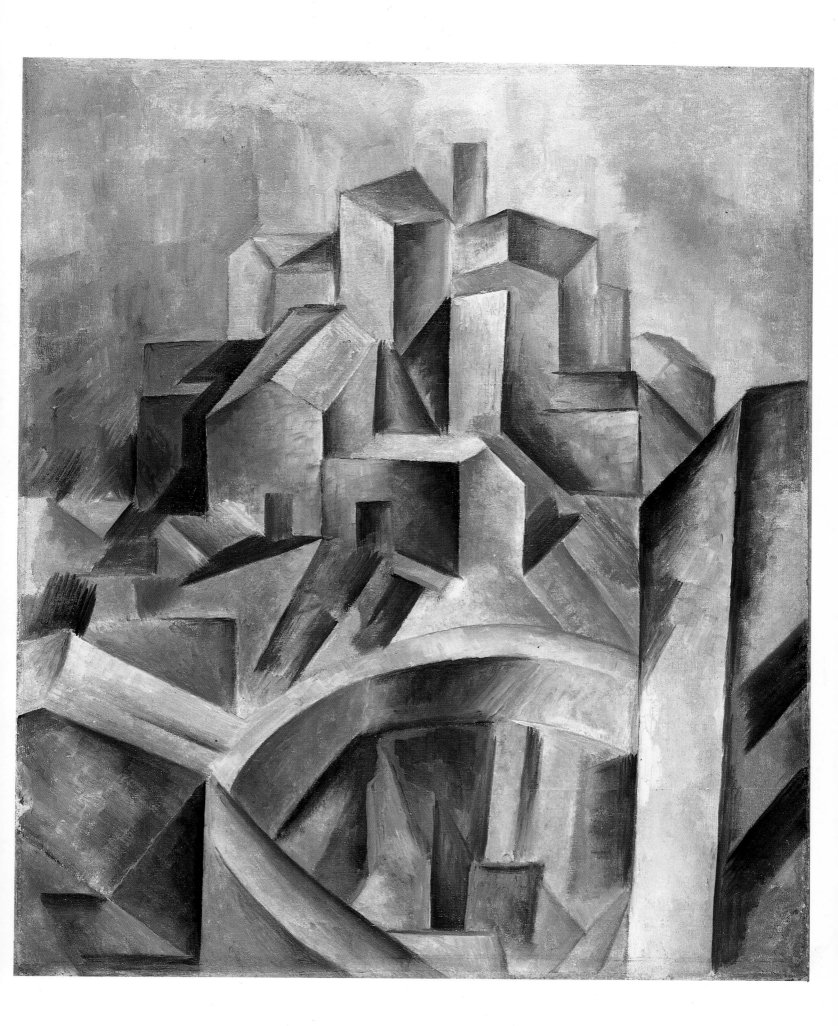

Painted 1910

PORTRAIT OF
DANIEL-HENRY KAHNWEILER

Oil on canvas, 39⁵/₈ × 25⁵/₈″

The Art Institute of Chicago (Gift of Mrs. Gilbert W. Chapman)

This portrait of Picasso's friend, advisor, and dealer is the most striking example of how the artist applied his newly created artistic language to the portrait; that is to say, to the characterization of an individual human being. It also shows what great progress he had made since the year before in mastery of the Cubist idiom, here handled with sureness and conciseness.

In 1910 Picasso went back to the human figure. Besides several female figures, he painted three portraits that year, in which he explores the potentialities of the Cubist style—his portraits of Wilhelm Uhde, Ambroise Vollard, and finally, this one of Daniel-Henry Kahnweiler, which shows most fully the new treatment of form. The work is at the same time a tribute to the man who not only helped him to sell his paintings but also introduced him to contemporary philosophy—a friend who recognized from the outset the importance of the Cubist idiom and then faithfully continued to defend it. Picasso's portrait of Kahnweiler would deserve to be included here if only for his considerable contribution to the development of Cubism.

In this work Picasso has gone a long way in the direction that he had taken when he painted *Les Demoiselles d'Avignon,* farther and farther away from the object, ever more concerned with consolidating the pictorial order. Here he is a long way, too, from the landscapes painted at Horta de Ebro in 1909, in which geometrical order predominates. In the portraits of 1910, especially this one of Kahnweiler, the artist puts his subject through a rigorous, unsparing analysis, breaking up the forms into their elements in a manner not unrelated to contemporary developments in the natural sciences. He breaks up the closed volumes, and arrives at a pattern of overlapping, tiny planes which evoke a three-dimensional plastic order similar to that of a faceted gem. In this shallow stratum of small, elementary planes superimposed upon one another (*plans superposés*), the head and hand of the sitter are individually characterized as centers of gravity. Details such as the watch chain are also incorporated in the pattern of facetlike planes. The colors—blue, ocher, and gray-violet—play a subordinate part; for here Picasso is primarily interested in the analysis of form, the systematic breaking up of volumes into their elements, an objective order of forms in space. He achieved this aim convincingly and masterfully in the portrait of his friend Kahnweiler, who sat for it about twenty times.

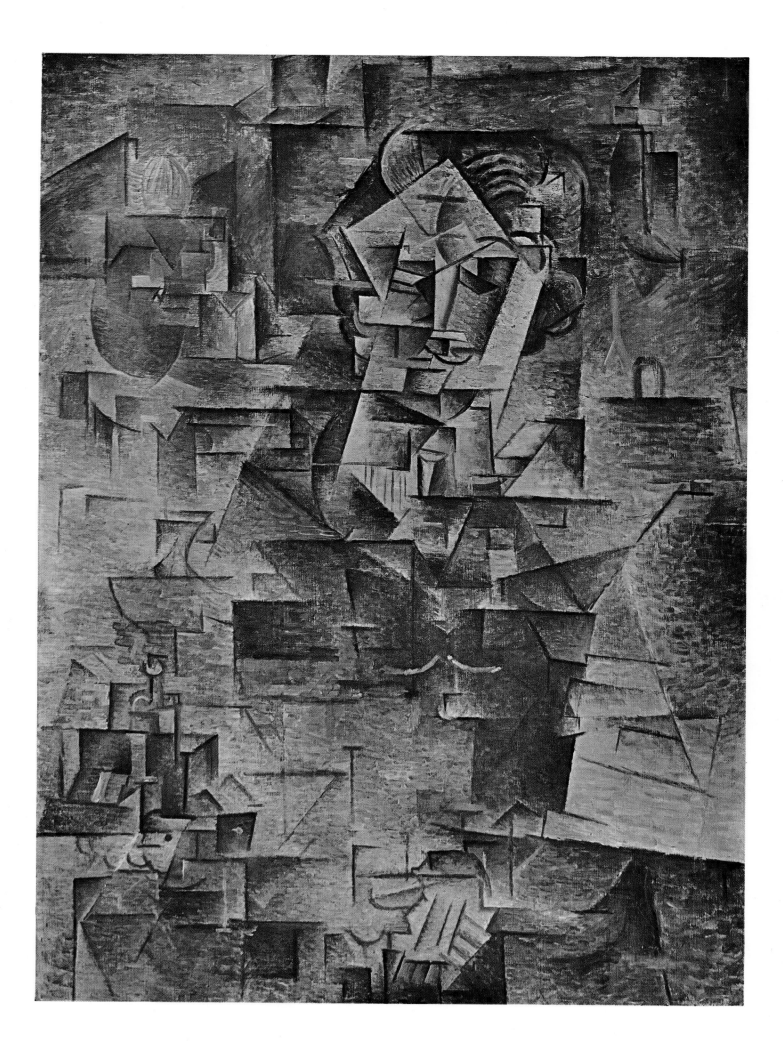

Painted 1911

MAN WITH A PIPE

Oil on canvas, 35³/4 × 27⁷/8″
Kimbell Art Museum, Fort Worth

During the summer of 1911 Picasso brought his Cubist style to a new peak in several large, firmly constructed figurative paintings. For these paintings he used a new, at that time unprecedented—truly revolutionary—format: the oval. About three dozen paintings dating from 1911 and the two following years make use of the new shape, which takes on compelling meaning from the inner structures of the works.

The works painted during the summer of 1911—which Picasso spent with Braque at Céret (Pyrénées Orientales)—continue the breaking up of bodies into facets, going farther in this direction than the works of 1910, including the portraits of Uhde, Vollard, and Kahnweiler, had done. This development may have been induced by Picasso's recent work with sculpture—including the woman's head in bronze (figure 15). Similarly, Picasso's interest in still life— which comes to the fore at this time—surely furthered his concentration on the architectonic structure of form. Whether it be a portrait, a still life, or a landscape, his subject seems much less important than the formal structure. In these paintings a powerful sense of the world's underlying unity asserts itself: man, things, and space are equally facets of a vast, architectonic reality, and the painting's subject is conceived of as an occasion for the artist to make a statement defining this reality. Each of these works, whatever its subject, is thus in its structure, in its syntax, a metaphor of the world's physical structure, the reality around us.

Precisely because of these fundamental innovations, the oval format takes on fresh and more comprehensive significance. The painting is no longer a segment of reality, but a world in itself, separate and self-contained. The Cubist compositions from 1911 on are turned in on their own points of focus, the effect of internal repose being ever more tightly knit. At the edges, the paintings are empty, the whole energy of each work turned inward to the center.

Man with a Pipe is no doubt the masterpiece, the classic in this series of works in which the crystalline structure of form achieves monumental clarity. The two pyramids of small, facetlike planes fitted into one another appear as one architectonic entity to the viewer. And yet, not all reference to objects has been sacrificed: the man's head, his shirt sleeves, the newspaper in his hand—such details have not just been reduced to a formula, but are still clearly "denoted," i.e., translated into legible signs. Color is there only for the sake of form: in this world, whose significance lies so completely in the structure of form, color plays a very subordinate part. The essential element in all these paintings is the statement made concerning the structure of reality, and it is only the austerity of the Cubist idiom, rather than the object, which has any importance in relation to it.

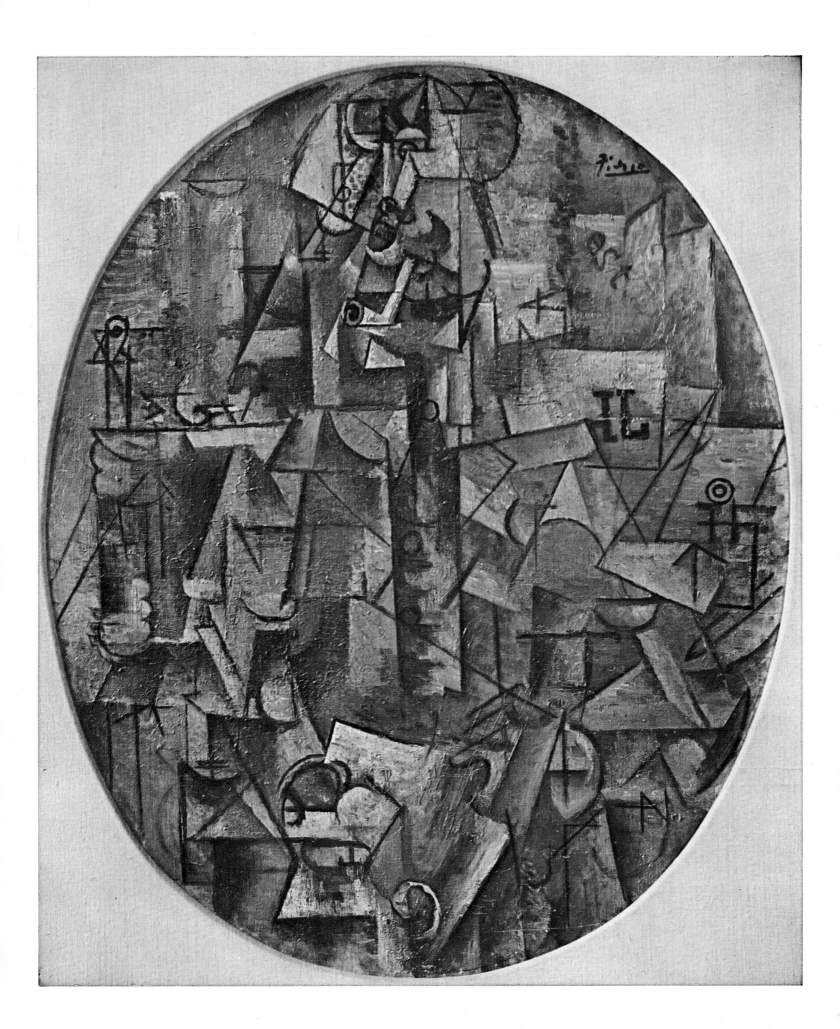

Painted 1912

THE AFICIONADO

Oil on canvas, 53¹/₈ × 32¹/₄"
Kunstmuseum, Basel

In the summer of 1912, which was spent at L'Isle-sur-la-Sorgue near Avignon, Picasso completed his development of that part of the Cubist style which aimed at breaking up form into its elements, and for this reason has become known as Analytical Cubism in the history of modern art. *The Aficionado,* which shows the figure of a man seated at a café table, is probably the most representative work of this period; in it five years of penetrating explorations are brought to their conclusion.

In this work, which is painted in restrained and subdued colors, we are immediately struck by the strongly vertical structure of the composition. It is based on a rigid system of vertical and horizontal lines, with the vertical axis clearly dominating. This distinguishes it from those works of the preceding years in which the compositional pattern was the oval or the lozenge. With this new system of composing in straight lines Picasso further stresses the depersonalization of his subjects; his sitters become mere pretexts for exemplifying methodically a rigorous grammar of form. The works done in the summer of 1912 show the same sternly logical coherence which characterizes the Latin language. They bring to mind the clarity and objectivity of Descartes' *Discourse on Method.*

In such a systematically balanced whole, a composition that derives its eloquence from the rigor of its intellectual discipline, Picasso incorporates the characteristic detail of the individual case: the hat, the little flag with the inscription "Nîmes," the collar and necktie, the carafe, and the newspaper with the title *Le Torero.* By such means he relates the supra-personal order, to which his painting gives form, to the everyday human environment. This fact shows that even during these years of high intellectual tension Picasso attached too much value to reality to banish it entirely from his works. It is significant that, although this is one of the works in which he helped pave the way for nonobjective painting, he never himself painted in that style.

His purpose in this period was not the creation of a nonobjective art, but the complete objectification and depersonalization of the object as a spatial fact in the real world. In the works of 1912 Picasso freed painting not from the existence of the object, but from its momentary appearance. The composition based on rigorous straight lines certainly contributes to this result; moreover the sensory charm of the object is played down by the subdued colors so as to emphasize the spirituality of the conception. Only in the brushstroke do we still find a shade of personality. During this same year Picasso was to find yet another new technique.

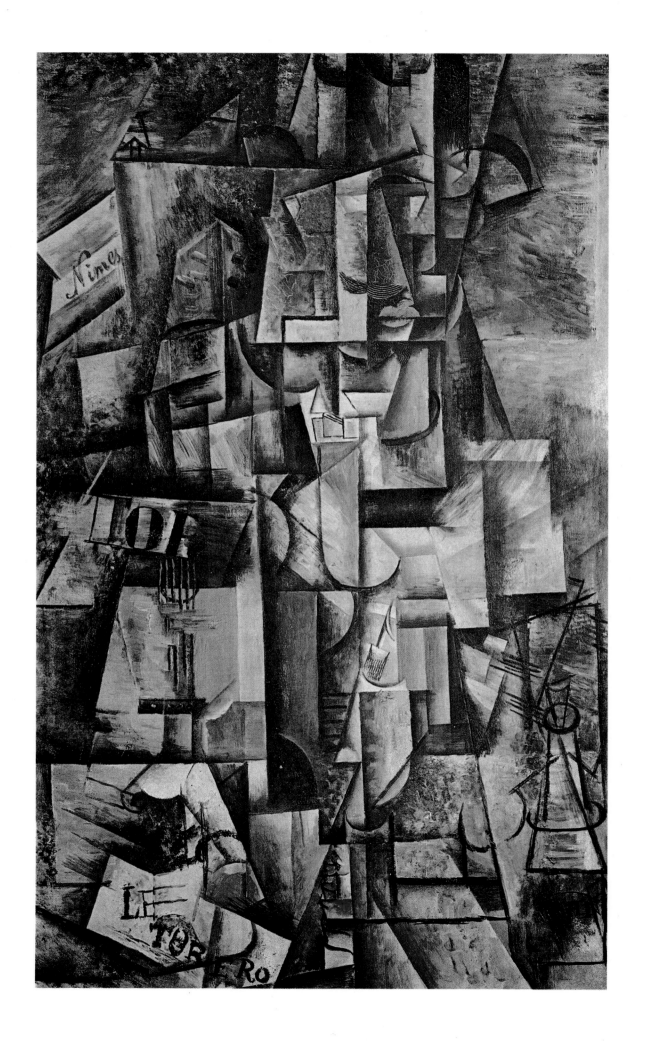

Painted 1912

BOTTLE, GLASS, AND VIOLIN

Charcoal and pastel paper, 18^1/$_2$ × 24^5/$_8$″
Moderna Museet, Stockholm

With the collages, or pasted papers, that Picasso began to produce in 1912, he embarked on the path that was to take him beyond Analytical Cubism. The composition shown here is perhaps the most accomplished and freest in this series of collages. It clearly illustrates the features of the new technique and defines the aims Picasso set for himself in these works.

What we have here is a still life based on the shapes of quite ordinary things—a bottle, a glass, a violin—and using actual pieces of newspaper. It is noteworthy that Picasso used this new style mainly for still lifes and, occasionally, heads. Here, once again, the problem of elementary form is at the center of his interest.

But the problem is treated in a fundamentally new manner. In the works of Analytical Cubism, Picasso reduced the forms to their elements; breaking them up into small components, into many facets, and using them as building blocks, he created a new order of things in space on the picture surface. By juxtaposing and interlocking the planes in short, rapid brushstrokes, he obtained a structure of crystalline clarity, reflecting rigorous intellectual discipline. Now, at the end of Cubism's analytical phase, he follows exactly the opposite procedure: the elements of form serve as starting points for works still rigorous, but at the same time much more lyrical.

Instead of breaking up forms into their elements, he begins with the elements themselves, transforming them into things—the ordinary objects of everyday life. And he achieves even greater objectivity by renouncing brushstrokes and the laying on of color; instead, the elements of form appear in his compositions as fragments of ready-made things: newspaper clippings, pieces of wallpaper, papers with printed veined-wood patterns, and the like. These fragments, borrowed from everyday reality, represent the world outside the picture and show that the composition can be so autonomous, so well knit, that it can even incorporate extraneous materials. In other words, as Kahnweiler put it, "He can do without his own skill at wielding the brush." Thus, a piece of newsprint at the left can serve for a bottle, and the paper printed like veined wood makes a violin. A few firm lines traced with charcoal complete the transformation and bring the extraneous materials together into a whole.

During these same years, poetry was taking a similar turn in its development, beginning to employ the most ordinary, everyday words (*les mots de la rue*) in poetic composition. This combination of the crudest reality with the most elementary, impersonal forms launched the next phase of Picasso's development: these pasted papers are the first step toward Synthetic Cubism.

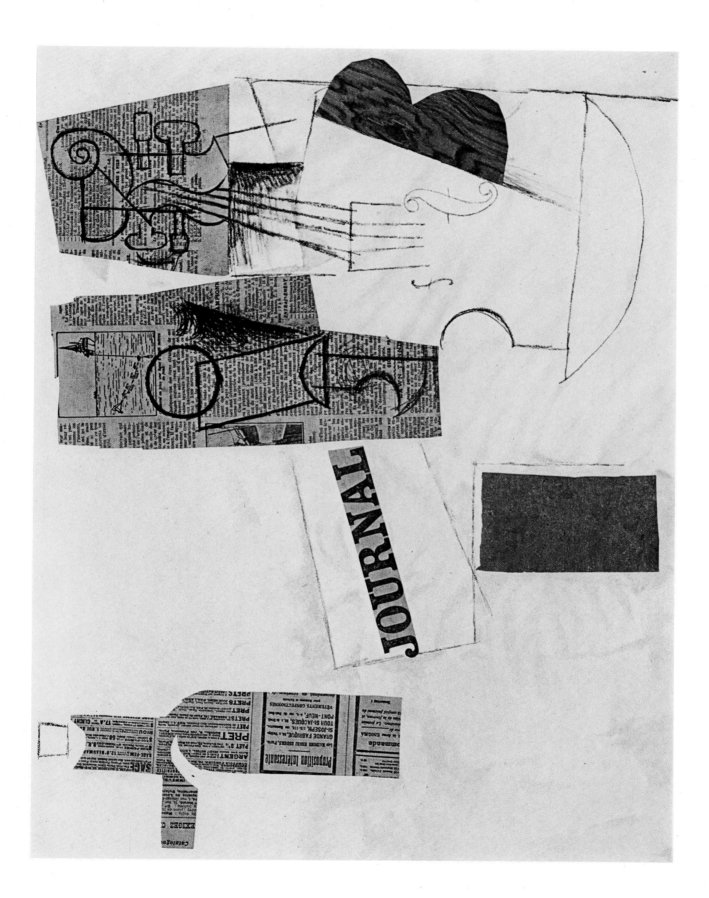

Painted 1913

WOMAN IN AN ARMCHAIR

Oil on canvas, 58¹/₄ × 39"

Collection Mr. and Mrs. Victor W. Ganz, New York

After experimenting with the new synthesis of form in still lifes incorporating bits of paper, Picasso applied in this monumental work his newly discovered formal idiom to the human figure. Here the real subject of the painting is no longer broken up into facetlike elements, but stated with great force in a new idiom.

Picasso treats the essential reality, whose transformed image is presented to the viewer, with the utmost seriousness. In his will to objectivity—which was at the center of his art throughout the Cubist phase—he supplies us with information about many details: the arm-rests and the tassels of the chair, the scalloped border of the shirt, the hair, and so on. But he is not interested in the outward appearance of things—he is aiming at their essential qualities. For this reason, just as he did in his earlier Cubist works, he avoids the one-sided contingency of perspective, and represents things not as they appear to us, but as they are, as we experience them. Thus he shows the chair not only in frontal view, but also as seen from above, and the breasts of the figure are shown both frontally and laterally, the two views being juxtaposed. By translating reality into this sign language, he achieves a new type of vision, a statement about the world of things which is no longer dependent upon the momentary, or accidental point of view. He makes a radical break with the traditional relationship between subject and object. Reality itself is at the center of this art, and the painter becomes the impersonal instrument of our cognition, our measurement of reality. A sign language made up of formal elements is employed by the artist to formulate his statement about reality as objectively as possible, to bring together all the object's characteristic details in a factual statement.

Precisely because of the hardness and objectivity of this vision of reality, the work has a dramatic quality that had not appeared in any of Picasso's earlier works. The immediacy of the statement untempered by any lyrical sensibility, the renunciation of an individual point of view, the objective sign language— all these characteristics of the work testify to a vision purged of the lyrical subjectivism prevalent at the turn of the century. With this vision, the artist is equipped to make a fresh conquest of reality, to report the artistic experience without bias or sentimentality.

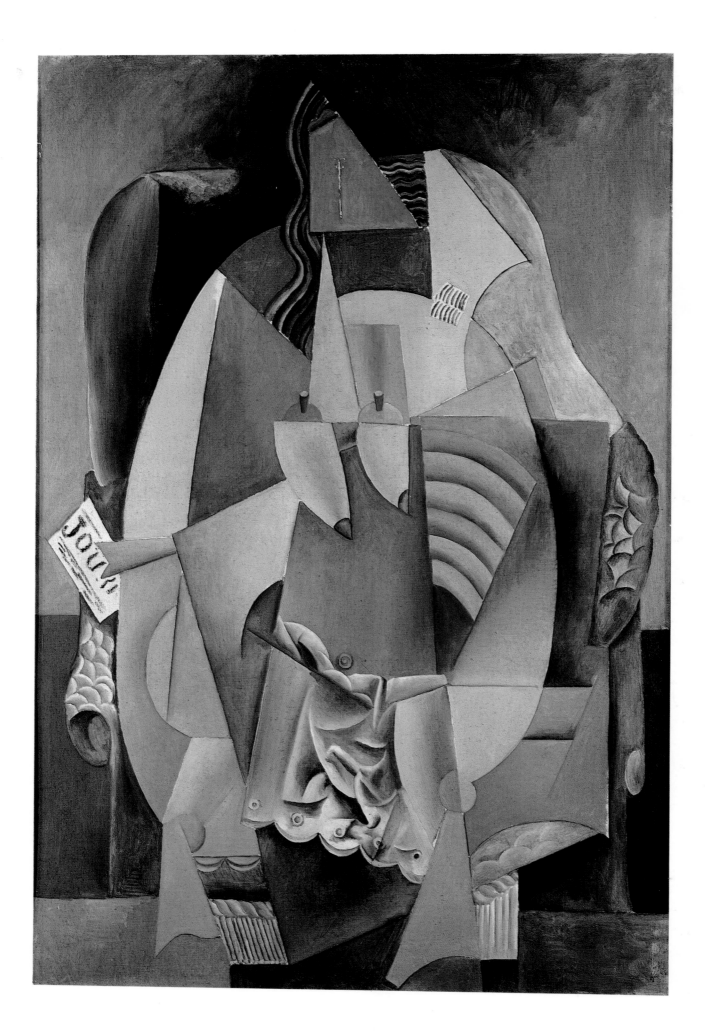

Painted 1914

VIVE LA FRANCE

Oil on canvas, 21³/₈ × 25³/₄″

Collection Mr. and Mrs. Leigh B. Block, Chicago

With this work Picasso resumed his series of still life compositions, in 1914. It stands in clear contrast to the dramatic austerity of his 1913 works: it is a painting of playful, casual cheerfulness. He executed it the summer of 1914, at Avignon, where he had gone with his friends Braque and Derain—his last summer in the country before the outbreak of the First World War. Like a few other works dating from the same year, this one conveys the carefree mood of the period—the last such summer Europe was to enjoy for several years to come.

It is not only the bright colors that strike the cheerful note; despite the rigorous over-all structure, the pictorial treatment of the forms is marked by many playful and witty ideas. We can scarcely be surprised that the term Rococo Cubism has been proposed to indicate the character of these paintings.

The witty idea upon which this still life of ordinary everyday objects is based clearly informed other new works by Picasso of 1914. The idea is simply to translate a collage into the traditional technique of oil painting. A number of details reveal this: the wallpaper pattern in the background, the playing cards at the left, and the way the bit of newspaper has been worked into the composition. It was an original idea at the time, and Picasso developed it painstakingly.

Moreover, the painting technique employed here derives from Picasso's experiments with pasted papers. Whole areas are treated with a pattern of colored dots, or they are coarsened by the addition of other materials, such as sand or sawdust, to the paint. These firmly outlined areas, because of their different textures, stand out as independent units, like the separate bits of paper in a collage; these, too, take on a new and distinct objective meaning, but without giving up their own consistency and "extraneous" character. It was by such means that Picasso—together with Georges Braque—endowed painting with a new dimension. The tangible treatment of the picture surface added new possibilities of expression to the sign language of Synthetic Cubism and greatly enhanced its attractiveness.

In respect to its over-all structure, however, *Vive la France* has more in common with the compositions of the preceding years than appears at first glance. Picasso is still very much concerned with creating an objective image of reality, freed from the contingencies of sense perception and yet capturing the essential features of the object represented. The sign language of Synthetic Cubism, which defines and explains reality with a few formal elements, made it possible for the artist, after the rigorous and dramatic works of 1913, to do justice to such sprightly, lighthearted subjects as the one presented here in *Vive la France*.

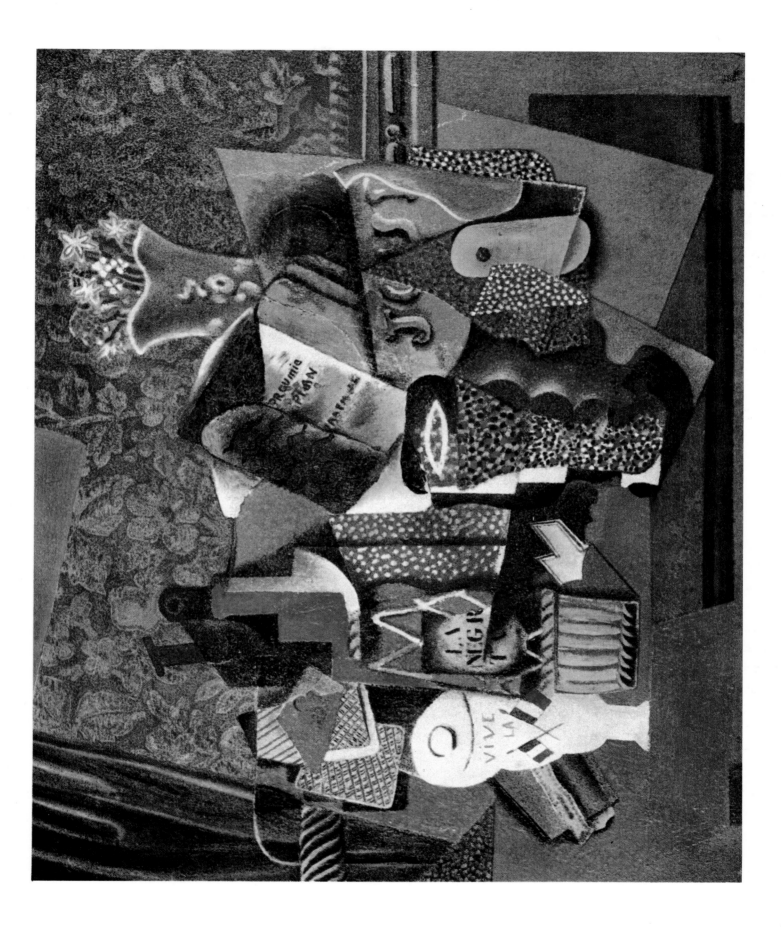

Painted 1918

PIERROT

Oil on canvas, 36¹/₂ × 28³/₄″

The Museum of Modern Art, New York (Sam A. Lewisohn Bequest)

After the systematic development of Cubism from 1907 to 1914, the series of paintings begun in 1917 comes as a surprising throwback. These paintings are entirely realistic in spirit—they seem almost traditional.

The return to the language of realistic art—i.e., sense perception as the basis for portraying reality—began as early as 1915, when Picasso made two strictly realistic portraits, in pencil drawing, of Ambroise Vollard (figure 19) and of Max Jacob. The masterful realism of these drawings aroused both admiration and indignation, but their production did not interrupt the evolution of the Cubist style. The figurative paintings of 1915 and 1916 are among the most accomplished of Picasso's strictly Cubist creations.

What then are we to make of the artist's working simultaneously in two styles, Cubism on the one hand, and the realistic idiom on the other? Had not Picasso abandoned the latter, back in 1906? It is noteworthy that at first he employed the traditional realistic treatment solely to portray persons with whom he was closely connected and of whom he was especially fond. He reverted to the earlier style, we may assume, because his models were psychologically close to him; they were part of his personal life, thus separate and apart from the objectively constructed works of the Cubist period. The realistic drawings and portraits are not really incompatible with the Cubist works; they are personal notations, a sort of diary that Picasso kept while his main artistic preoccupations were caught up in the exploration and conquest of a new reality.

The painting shown here is one of the most accomplished and most important of the series. During his trip to Italy with Jean Cocteau to design the sets and costumes for Cocteau's ballet *Parade* (which was first staged in Rome), he became acquainted with the *commedia dell'arte*, its characters and traditional costumes. As he grew to be more familiar with the world of the ballet (he married Olga Koklova, a dancer, in 1918), Picasso was inspired to execute a series of paintings and drawings which, like this painting, bring out a certain melancholy and other psychological aspects of the milieu in a newly developed realistic language of form.

The clarity of the drawing, the plastic treatment of the forms, and the brightness of the colors in this painting (as also in the portraits of the artist's wife and the drawings of friends that he did around this time) recall the classical works of Ingres; and their tight discipline reveals the underlying closeness of these works to his Cubist production, in which Picasso was reaching the classical high point during these same years.

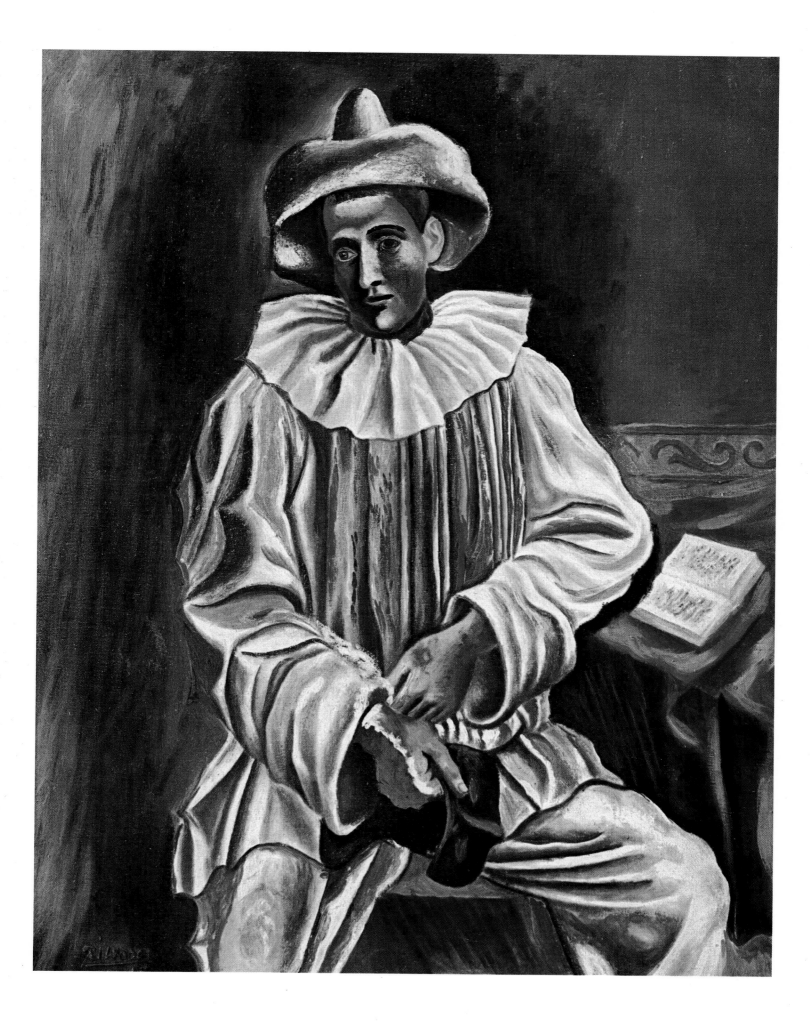

Painted 1921

THREE MUSICIANS

Oil on canvas, 79 × 87³/₄"

The Museum of Modern Art, New York (Mrs. Simon Guggenheim Fund)

Picasso painted the two versions of this large composition in Fontainebleau during the summer of 1921. Both versions, particularly the earlier one in The Museum of Modern Art in New York, must be regarded as the culmination of his Cubist style. After he created his first works in the style of Synthetic Cubism, his idiom underwent monumental simplification. Color, moreover, was at last assigned a role in the harmonious order of Cubist composition. Picasso no longer confined himself to pastel tones, but employed bright, primary colors.

Both versions of the painting show three figures—Pierrot, Harlequin, and a Monk, each of whom is playing a musical instrument. In this first version, Pierrot with the clarinet is at the left, Harlequin with the guitar at the center, and the Monk holding the music at the right. In the second version, which is in Philadelphia (figure 21), Pierrot and Harlequin have exchanged places, and Pierrot in his white costume is at the center. The first version convinces by its tightly-knit composition and its classical clarity; the second is more showy and more richly articulated, but lacks the striking conciseness of the painting in New York.

In these works Picasso summed up his experience of the Cubist period: out of simple, almost geometrical elements he has created a lyrically expressive group that is often loose in details, yet firmly composed.

The subject of the composition—three figures from the *commedia dell'arte*—was inspired by his work for the ballet during the preceding years. After *Parade* he had done the sets for the ballets *Three-Cornered Hat, Cuadro Flamenco,* and *Pulcinella*, all staged by Diaghilev. The atmosphere of the theater makes itself felt in both versions of *Three Musicians;* it is directly evoked by the contrasts in costume pattern, the crisp stenographic characterization of the figures, and similar details.

Picasso succeeded, however, in transforming these theatrical elements into a true painting by translating them into the language of Synthetic Cubism. Large simple planes articulate the work but they are repeatedly transformed into objective elements, so that their significance becomes clearly legible. Here and there—for instance, in the lozenge pattern of Harlequin's costume or in the Monk's beard—the treatment calls again to mind the technique of collage, which is indeed at the origin of this monumental composition. The forms and colors in this painting have become signs that not only serve to denote a reality but also convey a spiritual situation in musical terms. Not only by its dimensions is this work the masterpiece of Picasso's Cubist phase: the richness of his pictorial language was never so concentrated as here, nor its validity so clearly demonstrated.

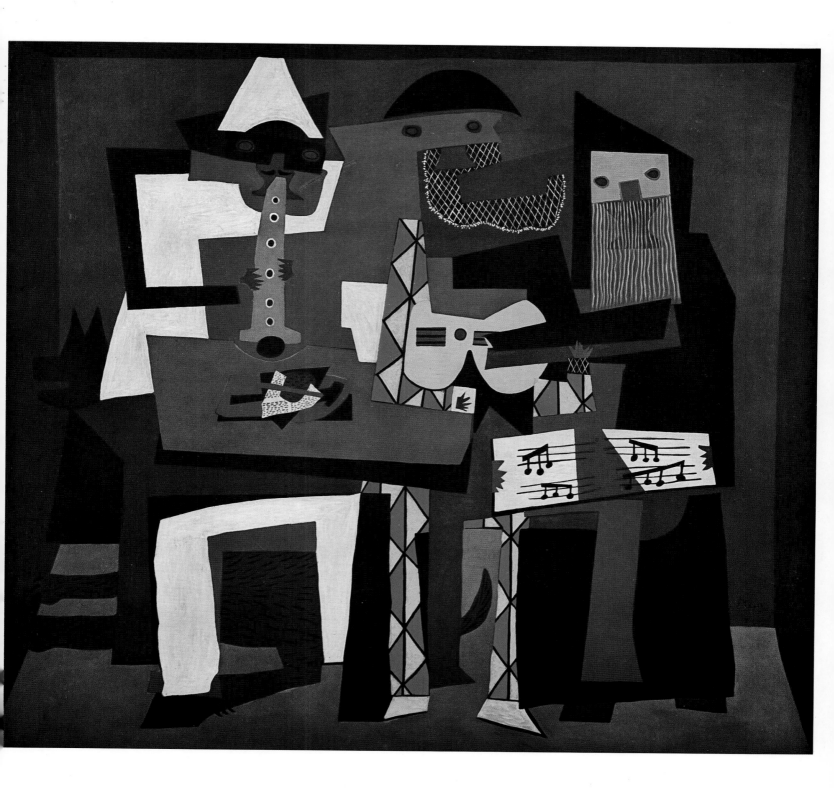

Painted 1921

THREE WOMEN AT THE SPRING

Oil on canvas, 80¹/₄ × 68¹/₂"

The Museum of Modern Art, New York (Gift of Mr. and Mrs. Allan D. Emil)

In the same year as the two versions of *Three Musicians,* compositions which truly evoke music, Picasso painted another large canvas in which three figures appear—three women at a spring. But the contrast between these works discloses the rich elasticity of Picasso's art: it is as though, between these big compositions, he were comprising the full range of his creative powers.

Both versions of *Three Musicians* are permeated with the spirit of music; quite apart from the subject, the treatment is thoroughly musical, and the effect of the paintings, especially in the first version, is that of a polyphonic work with contrapuntally interlaced themes.

There is no trace of the spirit of music, however, in *Three Women at the Spring,* of the same year. The inspiration comes wholly from sculpture, from the spatial properties of the bodies. In this work, into which the powerful bodies of three colossal women are compressed, Picasso harks back to his studies of 1906, that is, to the period when the plasticity of bodies, their three-dimensional existence, was at the center of his interest.

The artist's predilection for plastic volumes in the treatment of the human figure—which during the years of Cubist formal analysis had been set aside in favor of a different conception of space—was revived by a trip to Italy and the artist's contact with Roman sculpture. The "classic" phase which came about from this exposure to works of antiquity was above all inspired by sculpture. The treatment of the drapery in this painting brings to mind Roman sculpture, not to mention the fluting of Roman columns. Everything in the painting, including the subdued fresco-like colors, aims at the effect of volume, of majestic corporeality. There is no psychological interest exhibited in this composition: the artist has confined himself to representing the Arcadian, unproblematical presence of these powerful bodies.

This unself-consciously sculptural treatment no doubt reflects one feature of contemporary history: the relief experienced by mankind after the years of the First World War, the hope that a new Arcadia might be born from Europe's ruins. Always sensitive to spiritual currents, Picasso gives expression in this and in similar works to ideas very much in the air at the time. It is a masterful painting at the very opposite pole from *Three Musicians.* For some years to come, we will find him running the gamut between these two opposite extremes, as it were, of his inspiration.

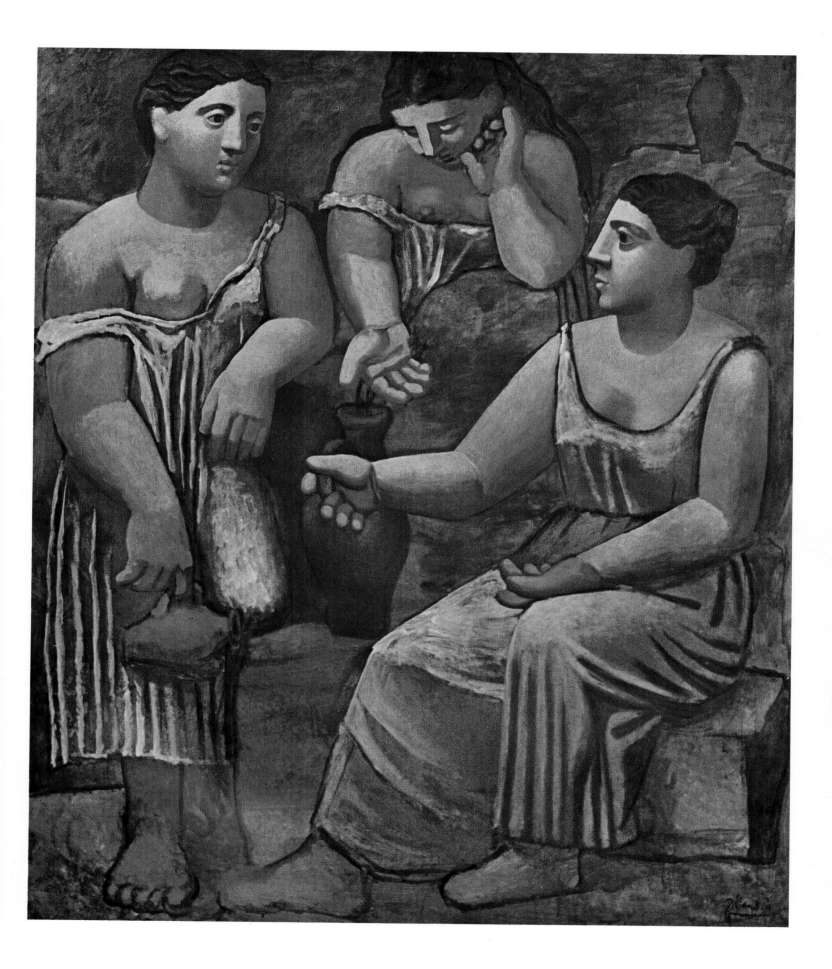

Painted 1921

MOTHER AND CHILD

Oil on canvas, 38¹/₄ × 28″
Collection the Alex Hillman Corporation, New York

The subject that dominates Picasso's work in 1921–22, and marks a new phase in his Classical style, is motherhood. In 1921 his wife Olga had given birth to their son Paul. The subject of the mother with the little boy thus arose naturally in Picasso's personal life at the time. He treated the subject in many paintings; this one is perhaps the most accomplished, the one which best illustrates Picasso's style in these years.

A typical touch is the impression we are given of larger-than-life dimensions. The figures of the young mother and the child do not seem to belong to the ordinary human race, but to some race of mythical heroes. This is achieved primarily by pictorial means: the figures fill the picture surface to such a degree that it seems almost cut off by the frame. The viewer has the feeling that the woman's forms are too massive for the size of the canvas, that they threaten to burst out of the picture. Body volumes and the pictorial space are here set in opposition, the result being exactly this impression of gigantic dimensions. This is further stressed by the contrasts among the colors, which range from pink to violet and from gray to blue-gray. Picasso here raises the subject of motherhood so far above his personal observation as to attain the monumentality of myth. To achieve this end he had only to draw on the Classical style which he had employed for the painting *Three Women at the Spring*.

The close kinship of both works may be seen in the gigantic proportions of the figures, the voluminous limbs, and the classical rigidity of the heads. The difference between the two lies in the psychological treatment: whereas the figures in *Three Women* merely express bodily presence and fill the canvas with their statuesque calm, those in *Mother and Child* are expressive of the artist's own participation in the action. Moreover, the figures are linked by internal relationships. The mother and child form a single plastic group, but their unity is not only plastic, it is also and above all psychological, emotional. This renewed interest in emotional relationships—renewed in the sense that more than fifteen years separate this painting from the works of the Rose Period—of course grew out of Picasso's personal life. Yet his work is never autobiographical in the ordinary sense of the term. He always raised personal experience to a level of universality and objectivity, as here, where the birth of his first son is rendered in terms of some perennial mythology.

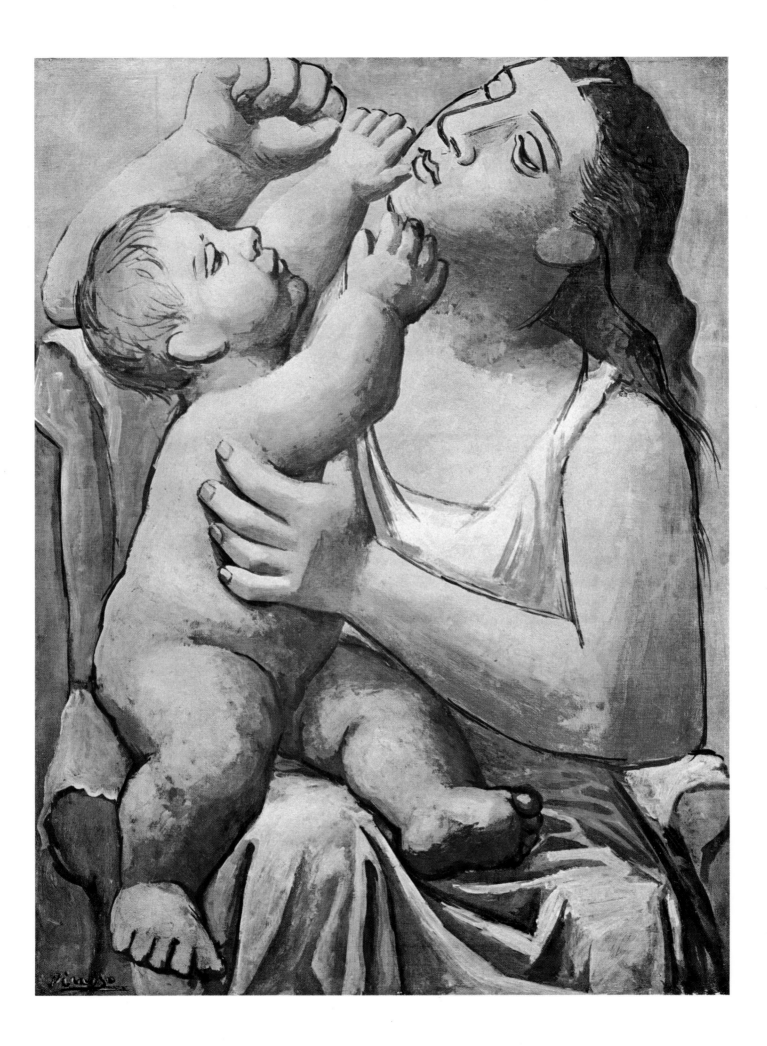

Painted 1924

PAUL IN A CLOWN SUIT

Oil on canvas, 51¹/₄ × 38³/₈″

Musée Picasso, Paris

During the early 1920s Picasso's production alternates between Cubism and a Classical style. Side by side with Cubist still lifes of the utmost structural refinement we find figural paintings in his Classical style, mostly with subjects drawn from mythology. A large number of drawings—usually pen drawings—also date from those years. In addition there are pictures of dancers and harlequins, often quite realistic, which testify to Picasso's continuing interest in the world of the ballet and the stage (which was especially kindled by his commissions for the Ballets Russes). Picasso had reached the age of forty and was now in full possession of his creative powers; the most varied impulses of his artistic will found their outlet in different styles.

In addition to these works, a new kind of picture begins to appear in these same years, and Picasso discloses yet another aspect of his complex personality: the portraits and sketches of his young son Paul. With them we discover a new facet of the artist's many-sided genius. These works lay no claim to raise or to solve new artistic problems: they belong wholly to the artist's personal life, and he kept nearly all of them.

Precisely because these works were not intended to solve any formal problems but were produced casually, almost playfully, they disclose the full breadth of Picasso's technical mastery. It is precisely in the works where his eyes and hands are freest that the richness of his creative ideas is most clearly and fully disclosed.

In the various portraits of Paul—in Pierrot costume, dressed up as bullfighter, or simply a child playing—Picasso shows his facility in handling composition, color, and the arrangement of space. As much at his ease as if he were making an entry in his diary, he places the figure and establishes its space on the picture surface, he animates the sparse harmony with some lively accent and articulates the large color areas with a few rapid lines or brushstrokes.

Looking at a portrait such as this, no one would suspect how much of Picasso's experiments with pasted papers, how much Cubist discipline has gone into these casually tossed-off little works. And yet it is these features that account for the portrait's sure mastery and raise it high above most artists' realistic portraits. Picasso's affection for his little boy is merely the painting's starting point; what makes it a masterpiece is Picasso's creative sureness.

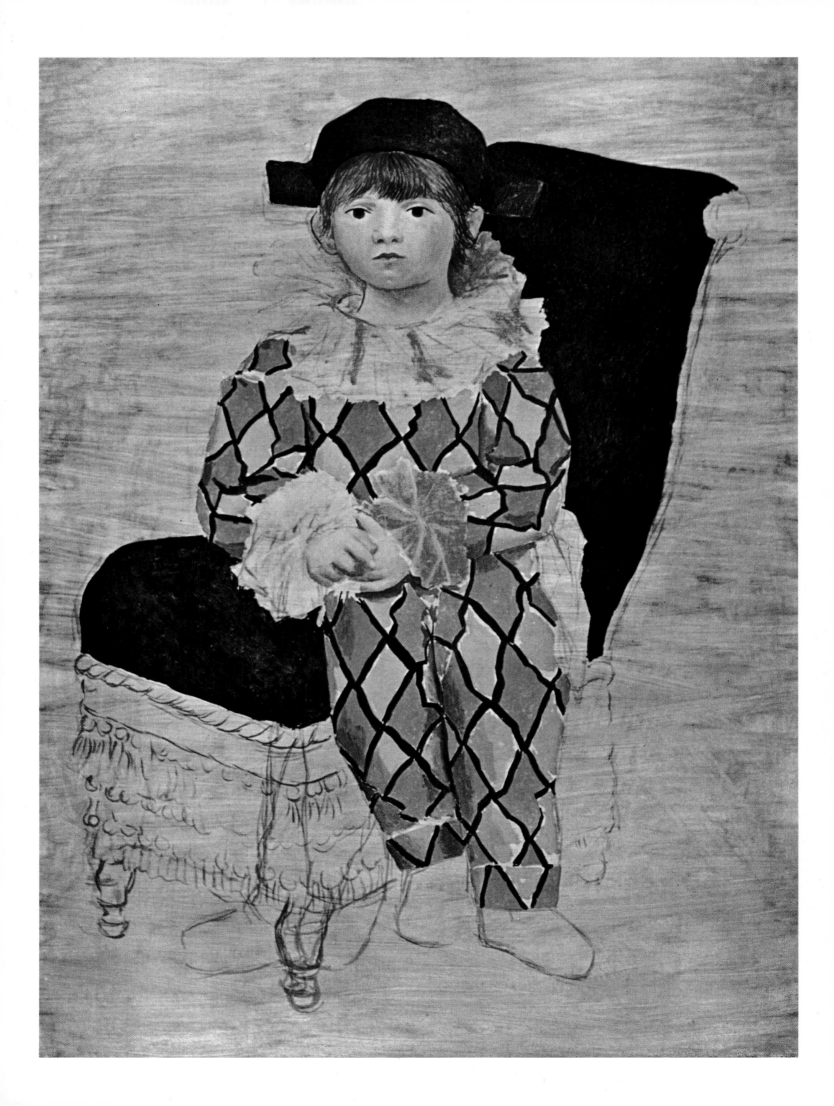

Painted 1925

WOMAN WITH MANDOLIN

Oil on canvas, 51³/4 × 35³/4"
Collection Walter H. Annenberg

Like the large still life of 1924, this work sums up a number of earlier experiments. Problems which had preoccupied the artist for many years are here given a classical solution. Even since 1910, that is, since the beginning of Analytical Cubism, he had occasionally treated the subject of a girl with a musical instrument—usually a mandolin or a guitar. The 1910 painting on this theme is one of the finest works of his early period, its rigorous structure pervaded with lyrical feeling (figure 16). This painting of 1925, too, achieves lyrical resonance, but in addition we have all the results of Picasso's postwar Classical style.

This work is surprising first of all for the composition—large colored planes articulated and animated by a few flowing lines. The harmony of three colors—tones of white, blue, and red—prevails, apart from a variety of tawny tones. None of Picasso's earlier paintings is based so completely on chromatic harmonies, and hence its musical quality is very different from that of the 1924 still life, where the compositional principle was the polyphonic interplay of different motifs. Here the triad of colors is self-sufficient and classically harmonious.

Here we have the results of Picasso's Classical style of drawing and painting, which had begun with his trip to Italy in 1917. He came back from Italy not only with a fondness for sculptural composition, as in *Three Women at the Spring,* but also with a need to express Arcadian repose, a quiet, lyrical harmony. The flowing lines that define the forms of the face and bodies also bring to mind Picasso's variations on themes from Ingres' Linear style.

However, the color arrangement—which after all constitutes the foundation of the painting—derives directly from Cubist compositions and collages. Here, too, the large color areas began as independent elements, only later transformed by the artist into objects. And just as in the pasted papers, the final objective accents are supplied with drawing.

What is new in this work—and almost unique in Picasso's career—is the chromatic richness of the composition with its large planes. It is through color most particularly that Picasso achieves this noble harmony, Apollonian in its serenity, all the more striking for the fact that in this same year Dionysiac passions were unleashed in the artist's work.

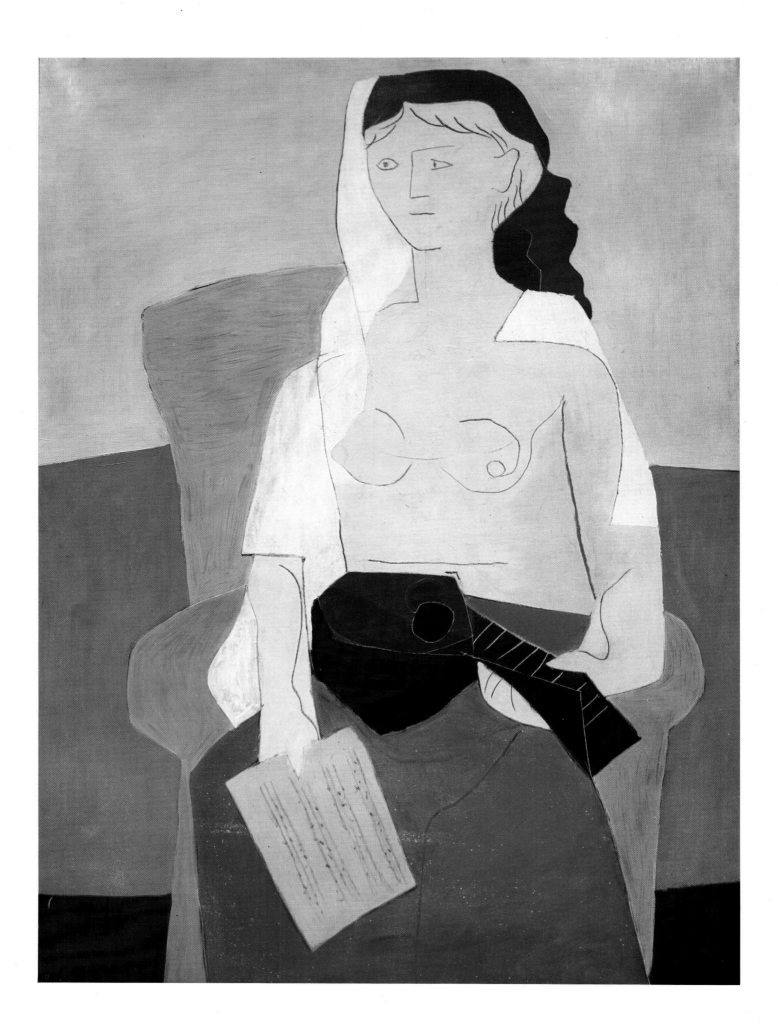

Painted 1925

THE STUDIO

Oil on canvas, $38^5/8 \times 51^5/8''$
The Museum of Modern Art, New York (Purchase)

Still lifes always played an important role in Picasso's work, but exactly at the midpoint of the 1920s they began to overshadow the rest of his production. It is in still lifes that the artist tests his means and records his achievements and conquests. The great still lifes of these years thus provide not only a survey of his technical mastery, but also of the whole range of his interests and problems.

The work shown here, sometimes referred to as "The Studio with Classical Bust," may almost be regarded as a summary of all that Picasso had learned down to this moment. Thanks to this work we can see clearly how he could go back to his Cubist style in 1925. The origin of a number of his pictorial motifs—above all his treatment of the tablecloth—in the collages of the years before 1914 requires no further explanation. The manner in which space has been made visible—and almost tangible—without resort to any illusionistic devices, likewise harks back to Picasso's intensive concern with spatial construction at an earlier time. The strong bright colors here disclose a more recent conquest: the new joy in color, which was first evidenced in the paintings (including some landscapes) executed at Juan-les-Pins.

This work, however, also discloses some features which do not reflect previous achievements, but rather point toward new possibilities in the artist's eventual development. Thus, the treatment of the bust in this still life clearly shows the combination of frontal and profile views. This method of suggesting volume will be much more completely developed in later works, in which the full complexity of the human face will be so vividly revealed.

There are other motifs here, too, that point to the future. For instance, the bearded classical head, which is the most important detail of the composition, foreshadows the interest in Graeco-Roman art and mythology which will come to the fore only in 1930, in the illustrations of Ovid's *Metamorphoses*. Finally, the fragments of arms and hands on the table with the head in this still life point toward the *Guernica* of 1937 where the same motif is very similarly treated, though with entirely different meaning.

This great still life of 1925 sums up Picasso's art at a crucial moment: past and future acquisitions are here found side by side. The juxtaposition of the carpenter's square with the branch of a tree should perhaps be interpreted along the same lines—namely, that the two symbolize order and growth, the two poles of artistic activity. The work sums up these two aspects of Picasso's art in a monumental synthesis, and at the same time it marks an essential turning point.

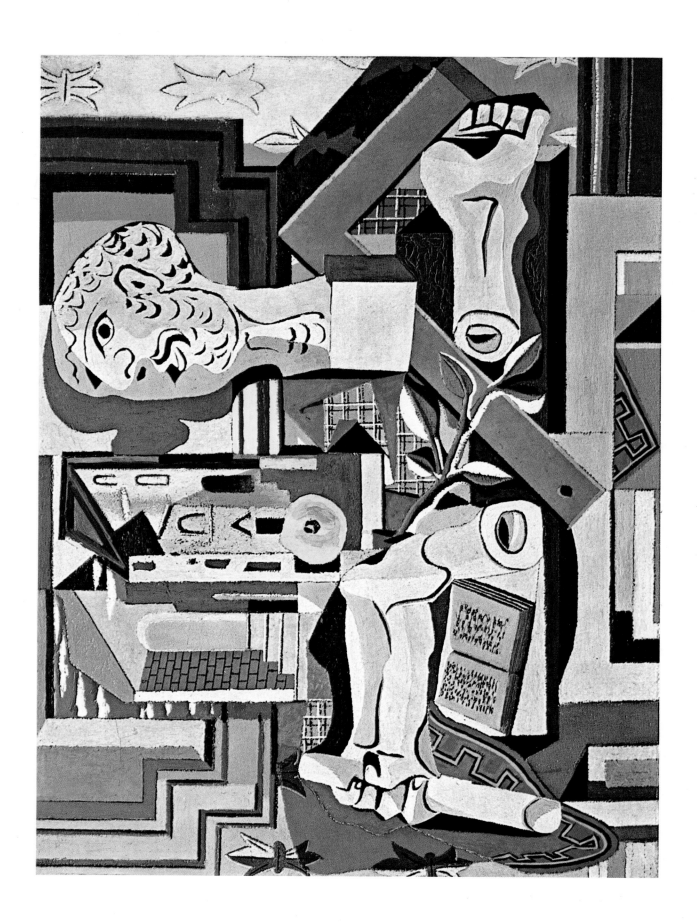

Painted 1928

THE STUDIO

Oil on canvas, 59 × 91"

The Museum of Modern Art, New York (Gift of Walter P. Chrysler, Jr.)

The subject of this painting—the artist at work—began to preoccupy Picasso in 1926. In 1927 he included it in a group of etchings with tense, delicate lines that bring to mind Ingres' drawings; this etching, together with the near-abstract ink drawings of 1926 (figure 23), was among Picasso's illustrations for Balzac's *Le Chef-d'oeuvre inconnu*, published in 1931.

In *The Studio* of 1928 the ideas present in all these earlier works are reduced to the simplest possible formula; simplification is carried still further than it had been in the *Atelier of the Modiste* of 1926, the motif being conveyed by a few lapidary signs. At the left of the painting we see the artist standing in front of a canvas, brush in hand; at the right is a fruit bowl and a plaster head on a table with a red tablecloth. A vertical and horizontal form—probably a window and a mirror—accentuate the back wall of the room; at the right is another vertical form, probably a door.

What strikes us first of all is that these objects have been translated into signs which have been completely integrated into the pictorial surface. The flatness of the painting is stressed by the light "frame" that surrounds the composition, thus continuing the pictorial surface beyond the actual composition, in the manner of a mural. *The Studio* also resembles a mural in that the forms are simplified and the colors reduced to a few strong tones—characteristic of a lapidary style. The work is not intended to be seen at close quarters but from a distance, as in a large hall or on a wall in a public square.

Such bareness and asceticism are exceptional in Picasso's works of this period, though there are many parallels in the paintings of Fernand Léger, Le Corbusier, and Ozenfant. At this time, these artists, too, were going in the direction of some more or less simplified mural painting. In the case of Picasso, this new spareness was paving the way for a new monumentality which, from 1929 on, was to take shape in projects for an actual monument. Contemporary with *The Studio* are other experiments with sign language, among them the wire sculptures (figure 26) which marked the return, after many years, of Picasso's interest in sculpture. All these departures are leading in the same direction: attempts to translate things into the terms of a kind of hieroglyphics, a concise system of magical signs.

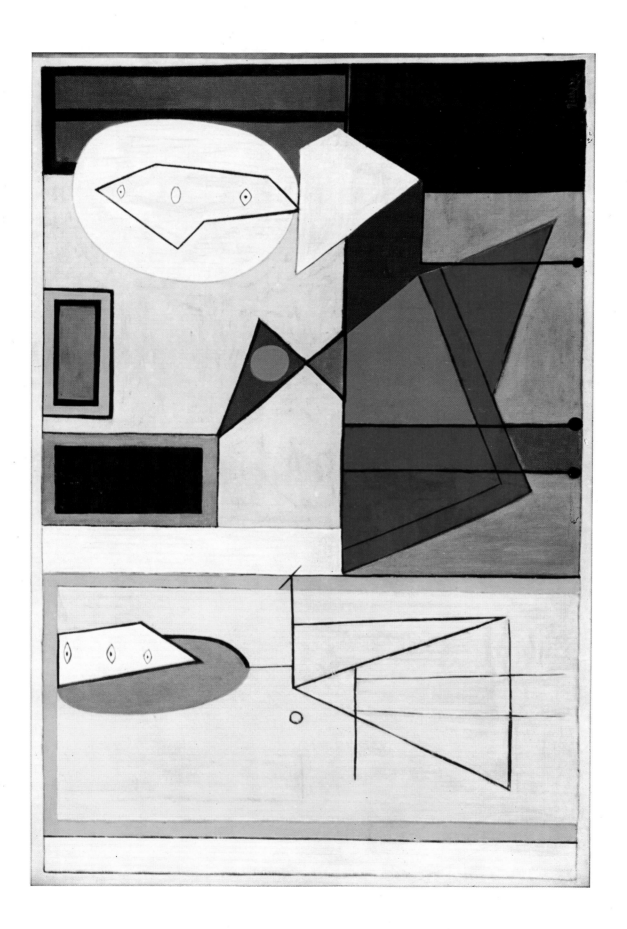

Painted 1930

SEATED BATHER

Oil on canvas, 64¹/₄ × 51″

The Museum of Modern Art, New York (Mrs. Simon Guggenheim Fund)

This work is an example of what has been called Picasso's "monster period." During these years Picasso was breaking away from the traditional conventions of human beauty, and explicitly creating an anti-image: man as monster, a dangerous, aggressive, destructive beast. In a few years Picasso's vision was to be given historical confirmation, but to his contemporaries the sense of these paintings was less apparent, and there are even today many who fail to grasp it.

The seated figure in this painting is one of these monsters. Though her forms are human, at the same time this woman is constructed like a machine of some substance both bony and cartilaginous. Her parts are jointed and hinged, they interlock and rotate around one another. As was to be shown only too clearly a few years later, this mechanized, machine-like quality is one of the attributes of human monsters who, once given the order to do so, murder, set fire, and destroy without compunction. Picasso's visionary gifts are obvious in these paintings and any viewer who looks at them today, remembering the recent past, must be amazed at how prophetically the artist stressed the aggressive features of the human organism, rendering it in terms of some demonic machine—the mouth that becomes a sawtoothed pair of tongs, the arm like a mechanical grapple.

Picasso began to demonize the human image as early as 1925, as he did in *Three Dancers*. But in that painting the human figure is distorted in the spirit of a Dionysiac orgy, an ecstatic drunkenness. What achieved unexpected expression in this and related works was deep instinctual forces: it was these which led to the first distortions and deformations of the human figure. Even then contemporary history may have been supplying impetus for the irruption of demonic powers into the artist's order-creating world.

Picasso's monster period began around 1929, when the danger of the triumph of barbarism and organized inhumanity first began visibly to threaten Europe. In these anti-images, a spirit of Dionysiac exuberance no longer prevails. These are stiff, mechanically perfect zombies which, like machines, are constructed to serve some specific purpose—in this case, that of aggression, destruction. Kahnweiler called Picasso the most humane artist of our time: again and again he proved his instinctive sensitivity to humanity's fate. In these works of the monster period, with their hard, bony forms and shrill colors, he for the first time spoke distinctly as a visionary, hence as a moralist. The language of these works was not at first understood, the critics preferring rather to take refuge in esthetic speculation than to grasp what Picasso actually had to say.

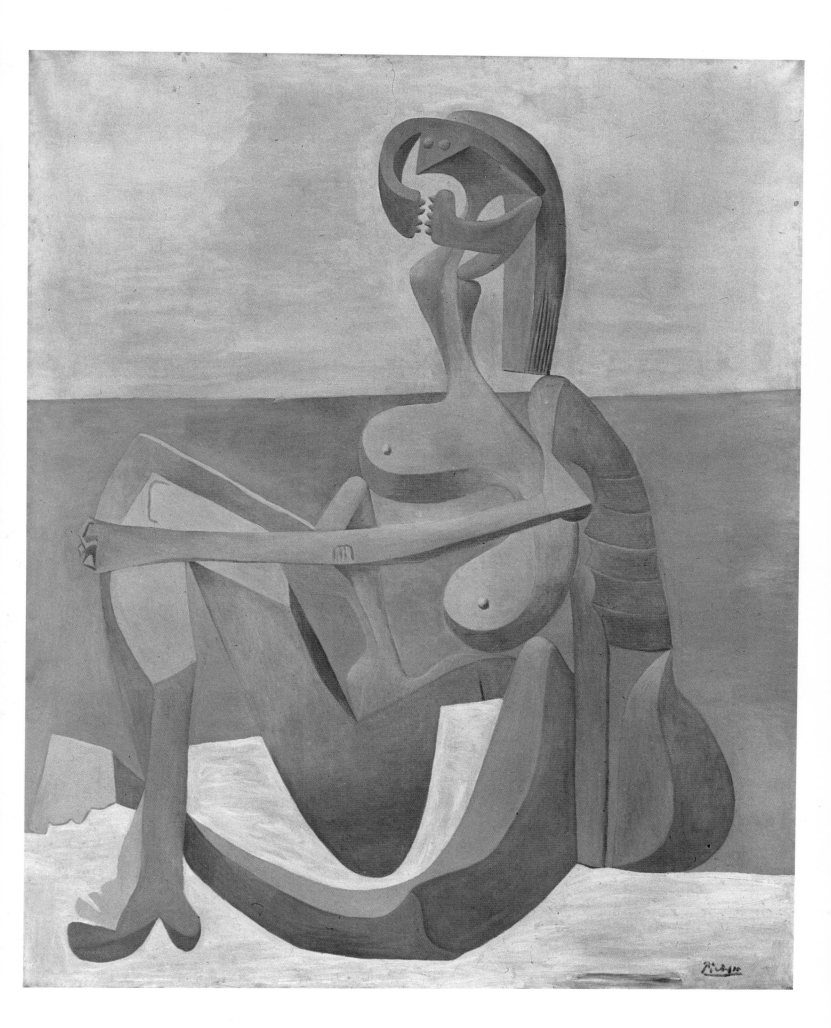

Painted 1931

PITCHER AND BOWL OF FRUIT

Oil on canvas, 51¹/₂ × 64″

The Museum of Modern Art, New York (Nelson A. Rockefeller Bequest)

In 1930 Picasso acquired the little Château du Boisgeloup near Gisors, where he devoted himself to sculpture, a pursuit he had mostly neglected since the Cubist days. His need for three-dimensional, plastic form was encouraged and aided by a friend of many years standing, the Spanish sculptor Julio Gonzáles. In the spacious rooms of Boisgeloup he at last could indulge this wish to his heart's content.

Sculptural themes had been turning up in Picasso's work for some years, but he had invariably solved the problems in terms of painting. Thus, in a series of sketches for a monument he imagined for the beachfront at Cannes, he transformed a colossal cube-like construction into a woman's head by adding a few accents: teeth and hair metamorphose geometry into figurative art (figure 24).

In the first sculptures created at Boisgeloup this spirit of transformation produces ever new plastic forms: heads made of pieces of steel plate, radiating the same magical effects as the sketches for monuments in the preceding years. Not until later will Picasso make those peaceful sculptured heads which have so unmistakable an affinity with the paintings of 1932 and their model (page 103).

The tendency toward compact forms realized in the sculptures of 1931 is heralded in a few paintings done in late winter of 1931. These are a series of still lifes—usually showing just a few ordinary household objects, pitcher, fruit bowl, etc.—of which the work reproduced here is no doubt the strongest. The forms of the objects are captured in a few broad arc-shaped lines, reminiscent of the leading in medieval stained-glass windows. Within this network of lines the colors acquire a deep harmonious resonance, a very special luminosity.

To be sure, these works hark back to still lifes of the early 1920s in which arc-shaped lines seem to have first appeared. But it is precisely the sculptural quality that makes the idiom here far more convincing: the formal unification gives the objects a solemn monumentality which anticipates paintings and sculptures of the following years.

Characteristic of all Picasso's art was the way his different activities influenced one another: sculpture influenced the large forms in these paintings, and other sculptures were in turn suggested by the paintings. Picasso's art was governed by the laws of organic growth; however often the technique may have changed, it was to him merely a means of giving his conceptions the most adequate possible embodiment.

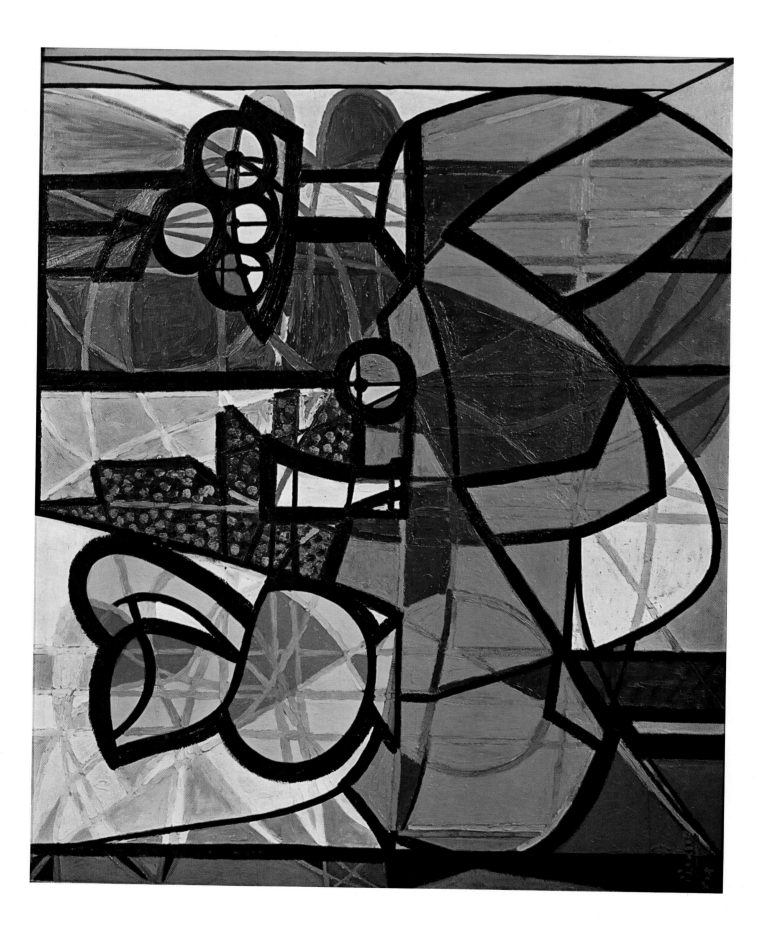

Painted 1932

THE DREAM

Oil on canvas, 51¹/4 × 38¹/8″
Collection Mr. and Mrs. Victor W. Ganz, New York

In 1932 Picasso began a new series of paintings: a sequence of female figures, mostly nude but occasionally clothed, almost all of them shown quietly asleep. The model for these paintings was a young girl, Marie-Thérèse, who three years later was to become the mother of the artist's daughter, Maia. Thanks to his new model Picasso found new tranquillity, in marked contrast to the mood that inspired the monstrous figures of the preceding years. The charm of these works is the greater for the fact that a fresh, naive sensuality pervades them.

The Dream, showing the figure of a young woman asleep in a chair, was one of the earliest paintings in the series; it is also one of the finest and strongest, perhaps because here the full sensual charm, the erotic appeal of this budding young woman, is so candidly expressed. Fresh colors and long, lightly drawn curves invest this painting with the effortless magic that characterizes many of Picasso's earlier works, but which he had not been able to achieve since about 1925, troubled as he was by problems both personal and worldwide. The effortless ease of this cheerful painting is not merely a subjective impression, it is a verifiable fact: the inscription on the back of the frame runs, "painted Sunday afternoon, January 24, 1932." The carefree mood of the work is tied up with changes in Picasso's personal life. The artist who for years had been brooding over world problems, now creates one of his warmest, most joyous paintings.

For all the rapidity of the execution, this is a masterpiece of balanced composition, extremely rich in pictorial invention. Surprising above all is the combination of the profile of the face and the frontal view into a convincing whole: the two views of the face endow the painting with spatial fullness and with flowerlike serenity. It is also fascinating to see how Picasso changes the colors of the outlines that define the various segments of the peacefully slumbering body: blue around the neck, black at the shoulders, then red against a white area contrasting with blue against a greenish area at the forearm. Contributing to the carefree mood of the painting is the dancelike gaiety of the lozenge-patterned wallpaper.

Closely related to this series of paintings is a series of large modeled bronze heads. They are pervaded with a similar plantlike vitality, and characterized by the same warm plastic fullness. Picasso created them at the little château of Boisgeloup, where he devoted himself primarily to sculpture.

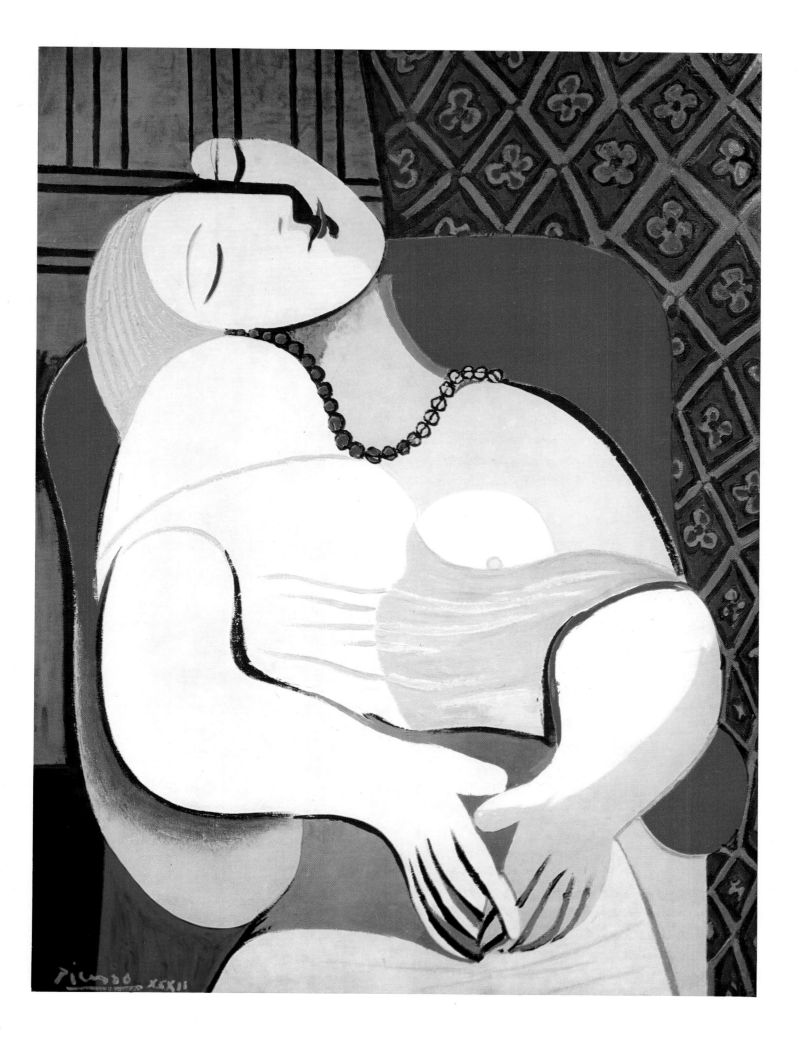

Painted 1934

BULLFIGHT

Oil on canvas, 38¹/₄ × 51¹/₄"
Private collection

In 1933 Picasso made a brief trip to Barcelona, and the following year he went back to Spain for a longer stay. Besides Barcelona, on this trip he also visited Madrid and Toledo. Impressions from these trips to Spain survive in a number of works on bullfight themes which he executed at Boisgeloup. In composition and color, the work shown here is perhaps the most striking of the series.

Picasso had been familiar with the bullfight from youth. As a subject, it turns up in his work as early as 1901, in a painting that almost impressionistical- ly subordinates the dramatic action to the atmospheric sweep of the arena— half in blue shadow, the other half in glaring sunlight. Subsequently, the bull- fight occurs again and again, either as main or subsidiary subject—for in- stance, in the sketch for the curtain of the ballet *Le Tricorne,* executed in London, 1919, as well as the 1927 etchings for Balzac's *Le Chef-d'oeuvre inconnu.* However, in the work shown here the bullfight is treated quite differently. We see the beginning of a development which will reach its climax three years later in *Guernica* (figure 34).

In the history of Picasso's art this 1934 painting, and the paintings and draw- ings related to it, mark a first step toward the creation of a wholly personal mythology which he worked out for himself during the 1930s. As early as 1930 we find him treating a number of traditional mythological themes, most notably in the illustrations to Ovid's great poem *Metamorphoses.* A *Crucifixion* dating from the same year is further evidence of search for a thematic form capable of embodying dramatic ideas. In 1934, at the same time as such bull- fight works as this one, Picasso produced etchings and lithographs for Aristo- phanes' *Lysistrata.*

In the theme of the bullfight, since his trip to Spain and its renewal of child- hood memories, Picasso saw a mythological symbol capable of embodying dramatic suffering, grief, and rage—capable of expressing, that is, the very feelings which were boiling in him in these years. Everything in the 1934 painting is focused on the dramatic clash between the black bull and the light- colored horse. The arena and the features of the spectators are only suggested, serve merely to frame the action. The drama of ferocious struggle has become the theme not only of this painting, but of the whole world of Picasso's imagination. These shrill contrasts of form and color evoke the manner he will employ in reacting to the events of the next few years: they anticipate the rage, the grief, the despair with which he will greet Fascism's ever more stultifying victory over the human spirit. With *Guernica,* in 1937, historical events will have caught up with such anticipations as those expressed in this work and its theme.

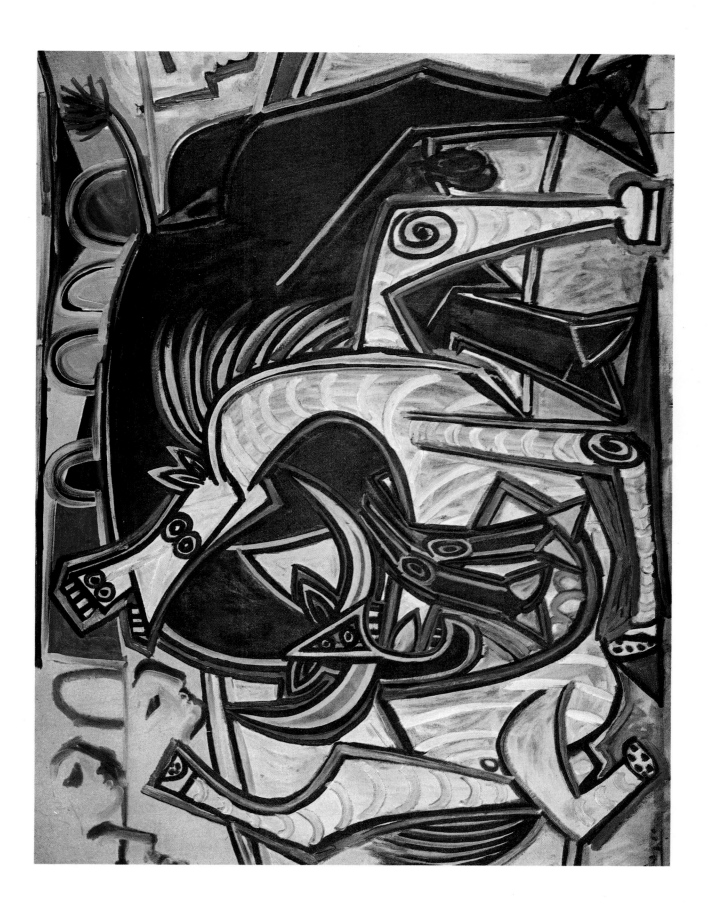

Painted 1935

YOUNG WOMAN DRAWING

Oil on canvas, 51¹/8 × 76³/4″

Musée National d'Art Moderne, Centre National d'Art et de Culture Georges Pompidou, Paris

In the early 1930s, along with sculptures and the series of sleeping nudes, Picasso was preoccupied with a new theme: a highly personal approach to mythological subjects. *Young Woman Drawing* falls into this very loose thematic category, within which Picasso developed a new and expressive style.

He had first treated mythological themes in 1930 when he illustrated Ovid's *Metamorphoses* with etchings done in a nervous, rhythmic linear style. That same year he painted a small *Crucifixion:* the style of this painting, with its dramatic distortions, points to a new Expressionist tendency in Picasso's art. By contrast, his illustrations for Aristophanes' *Lysistrata* are etchings in the Neo-Classical linear style, whose witty elegance is so appropriate to the text.

His explorations into biblical history and classical mythology have in common an attempt to discover an emotionally charged symbolic language suitable for expressing contemporary events and the artist's own experiences. Given the extremely personal character of Picasso's vision, mythology too had to take on a personal form, and hence, to be more than mere convention.

Picasso's personal mythology evolved through fusing themes drawn from mythology with more personal themes—especially the bullfight, which Picasso rediscovered during his trip to Spain in 1934. Thus he created the figure of the Minotaur to serve as symbol for the disaster hanging over Europe in the 1930s. Also into this category falls the series of drawings showing the sculptor in his studio, with overtones of classical mythology.

Young Woman Drawing belongs to the same group of themes. It originated in a number of paintings showing girls reading, writing, or drawing. Here too Picasso tends to endow even the subject chosen apparently at random with mythological significance and archetypal implications.

The vehement colors, based on a harmony of green, violet, and blue, like the monumental treatment of the figures and the space, make this painting one of the major works of the 1930s. It is also the last important painting of the early 1930s. For personal reasons Picasso had no opportunity to paint after this; in 1935 he brought out his first efforts at writing poetry. However, he was jolted out of his depression by an event that soon concerned all of Europe, but first only his native land—the outbreak of the Spanish Civil War in the summer of 1936.

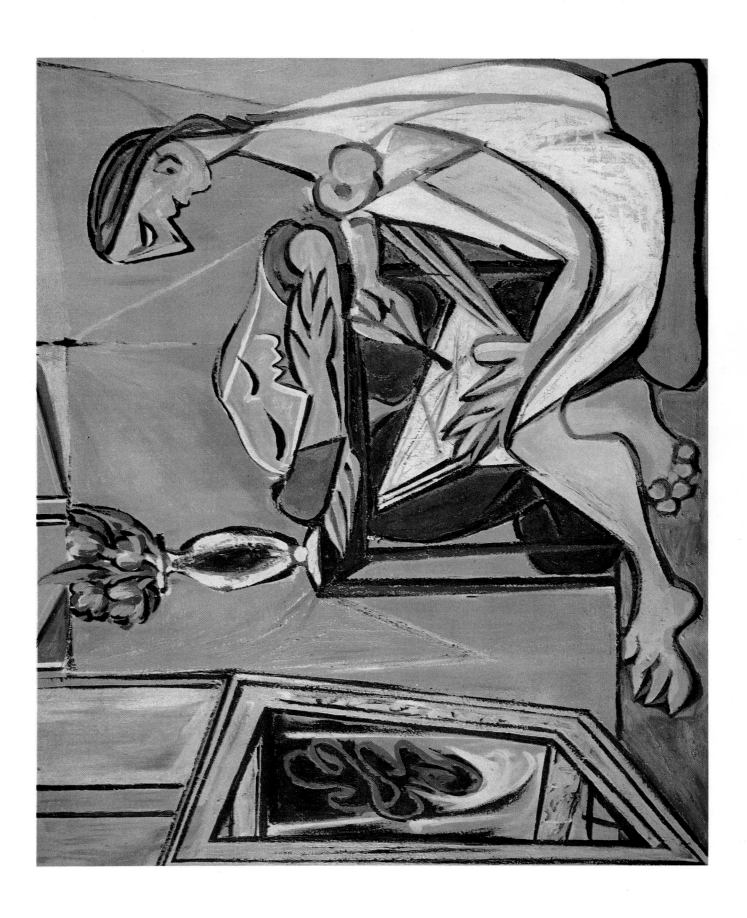

Painted 1937

WEEPING WOMAN

Oil on canvas, 23⁵/₈ × 19¹/₄″

Private collection, England

Weeping Woman belongs to the same thematic group as *Guernica* (figure 34), that monumental work which Picasso painted in the spring of 1937 under the direct impact of news that a peaceful little Basque town had been bombed by Nazi planes coming to General Franco's assistance. There is a weeping woman in the very first preliminary sketch for *Guernica*—it is the figure ultimately at the left in the painting, holding her dead child in her arms. In the final version this figure has been somewhat changed, but the expression of heart-rending grief so fascinated the artist that, after completing the large composition, he picked out this very detail for separate treatment several times.

Guernica was the crowning point of Picasso's efforts to create a contemporary mythology. This enormous painting composed with such convincing sureness was executed in a very short time. In January 1937 the Spanish Republican government commissioned Picasso to paint a mural for its pavilion at the Paris World's Fair to be held that summer. Before Picasso had produced so much as a sketch, on April 28 the whole world learned of the bombing of Guernica by the Germans—the first of those acts of senseless, inhuman, mass destruction that were, in the next few years, to demolish other cities in other countries. This event at once fired Picasso's imagination, and he poured out his bitterness and indignation in the first sketches for *Guernica,* dated May 1, in which the main lines of the composition are already clear. During work on the mural Picasso changed many details, but the painting has fully preserved the fire and dramatic impulse of the initial emotion.

Picasso expressed his bitter, savage fury over this atrocious deed in an extremely rigorous composition. The mythical figures are linked with each other within a triangular form that brings to mind the pediment of a Greek temple. Apocalyptic events take place within this area—the scream of the mortally wounded horse, the fear of the woman in the burning house, the agony of the warrior with the broken sword, and, at the left, the weeping woman. The austere palette, confined to black, white, and a few shades of gray, accentuates the impression of paralyzing terror.

To this magnificent work, inspired by contemporary history yet far transcending any one occurrence, *Weeping Woman* is a "postscript," as Alfred H. Barr, Jr., has called it. And yet this detail, transformed into a self-sufficient composition, contains all the apocalyptic mood of *Guernica*. The handkerchief which the weeping woman is biting in her boundless grief is a later invention that adds to the hectic vehemence of the expression. In one respect the picture differs from *Guernica*—in the strident dissonance of the colors. They help to elevate the dramatic conflict to the timelessness of myth.

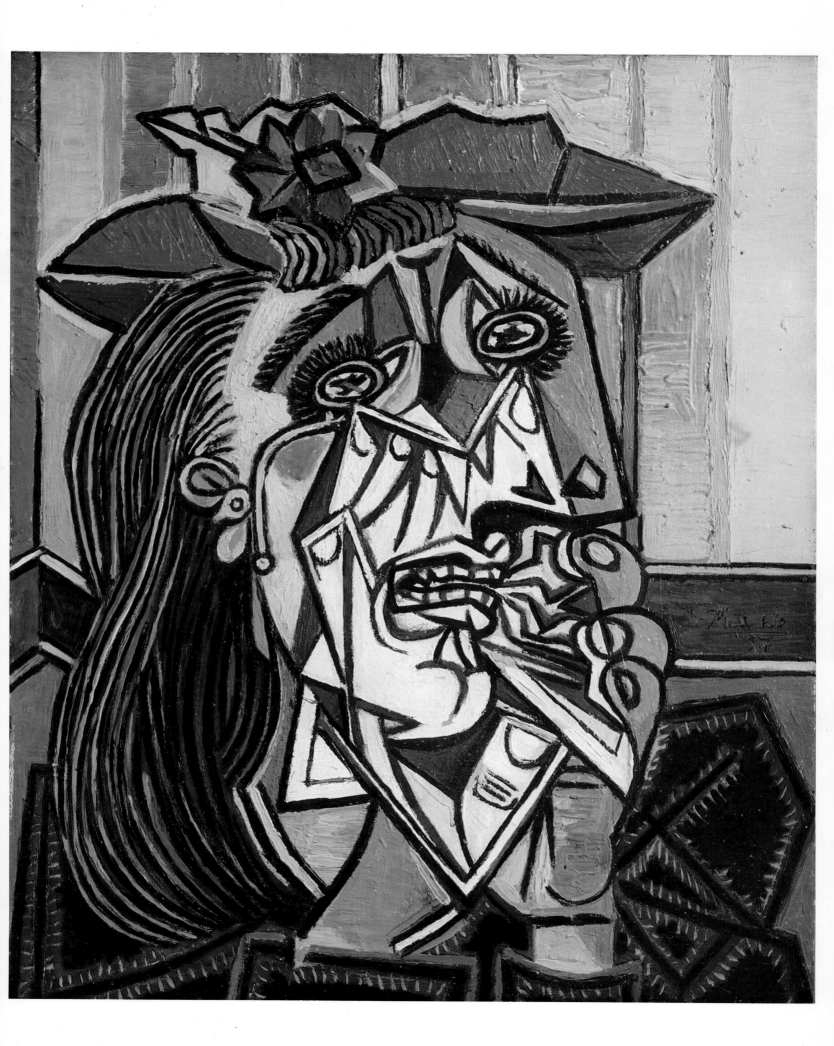

Painted 1938

GIRL WITH COCK

Oil on canvas, 57^1/$_4$ × 47^1/$_2$"

The Baltimore Museum of Art (Mrs. Meric Gallery Collection)

Even with paintings such as *Guernica* and *Weeping Woman* Picasso was unable to rid himself of rage at the inhumanity of the Spanish Civil War. His grief and anger, expressed above all in *Weeping Woman*, were not dispelled, but turned to disappointment and gloom when the downfall of the Spanish Republic became apparent.

In the course of 1938 he painted a number of works which give expression to his bitterness at the triumph of injustice; none, however, alludes directly to the events. That year Picasso went back to the themes of his monster period; he deforms and distorts the image of man in response to humanity's own self-debasement through committing injustice or failing to intervene in the cause of justice. Picasso's paintings of 1938 portray this debased humanity.

This work shows a girl holding a rooster in her lap, which she is preparing to kill. It is perhaps the most terrifying of the 1938 paintings, not only because of the violent distortions of the human face and body, but because of the solemnity with which a kind of sacred rite is being performed. Once again Picasso—who rejected any symbolic interpretation of this work—showed himself the clear-sighted interpreter of his time, and even of the future. In the years of terror that were approaching, it was precisely the seriousness, the conscientiousness with which the most loathsome atrocities were committed, that gave the deeds so especially sinister a character.

Thus *Girl with Cock* stands out among the works of 1938; it is more terrifying than the others, though most of them strike us in their harsh, merciless distortion. The portraits of the peasants of Mougins (where Picasso spent the summer), shown sucking lollipops, are pervaded with bitter irony and a demonic, self-tormenting anger (figure 35).

The impression of debased humanity, produced by the violent dismemberment and disrespectful piecing together of human forms, is strengthened by the shrill dissonance of the colors: the juxtaposition of pinks, greens, and blues has a provocative, bewildering effect. The sagacious observation of Meyer Schapiro, who discovered a similarity between the girl's head and Picasso's profile, may help us interpret this painting: Picasso identified himself—even though indirectly—with the tragedy and crisis of his epoch.

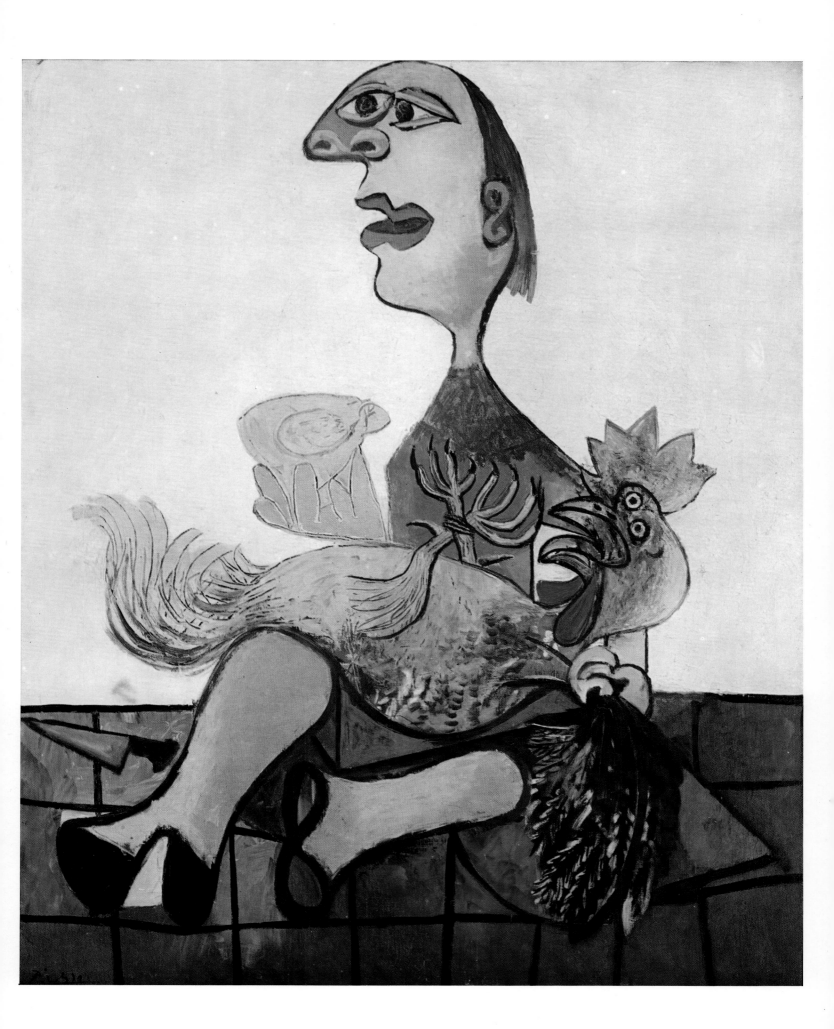

Painted 1942

WOMAN WITH FISH HAT

Oil on canvas, 39¹/₂ × 32″
Stedelijk Museum, Amsterdam

At the beginning of the war Picasso was urged to go to the United States or Mexico, but he refused, and early in the fall of 1939 he moved back to Paris from Royan (near Bordeaux), where he had been staying. He stayed in Paris until the liberation, working in the greatest seclusion. Curiously enough, the army of occupation left him alone, though he was forbidden to exhibit.

During the years that Picasso passed in a kind of voluntary imprisonment, he put all his energies into his work. He went back to sculpture, painted a number of large figural canvases and still lifes, and wrote a Surrealist play, *Le Désir attrapé par la queue* (*Desire Trapped by the Tail*). It was staged in 1944, shortly before the liberation, at the home of Michel Leiris, for a small audience of friends.

The most characteristic works of the war years, besides the still lifes, are the numerous paintings of a woman seated in an armchair. Although the theme is treated with many variations, almost all these paintings show a woman seated in a narrow space, often identifiable as a corner of Picasso's studio in the Rue des Grands-Augustins. In all of them the woman is represented as a bust or half-length figure, invariably with the hands showing.

The work reproduced here stands for a number of similar paintings. Some features are common to all of them: the figure always seems to be squeezed into her chair, as though imprisoned in an iron cage. In all of them the summarily treated body contrasts strikingly with the face which is painted in a new and original manner. To this last-named feature the paintings owe their gripping psychological effect, one of emotionally charged aggressiveness.

This particular work adds another feature to the series: Picasso transforms the woman's hat into a fish, adding knife and fork and lemon. This is a kind of grim humor which aptly characterizes the artist's mood during the war years. We may have here an allusion to the scarcity of food in occupied Paris.

In the same year Picasso demonstrated his amazing ability to change objects into the forms of a sculpture. In the *Bull's Head,* made of the handlebars and seat of a bicycle (figure 38), Picasso achieves the magical effect of the Negro masks which he had used for models as long before as 1907: the elements of form yield a meaning that is directly grasped by the viewer. During the war years Picasso rediscovered the magic power of his art.

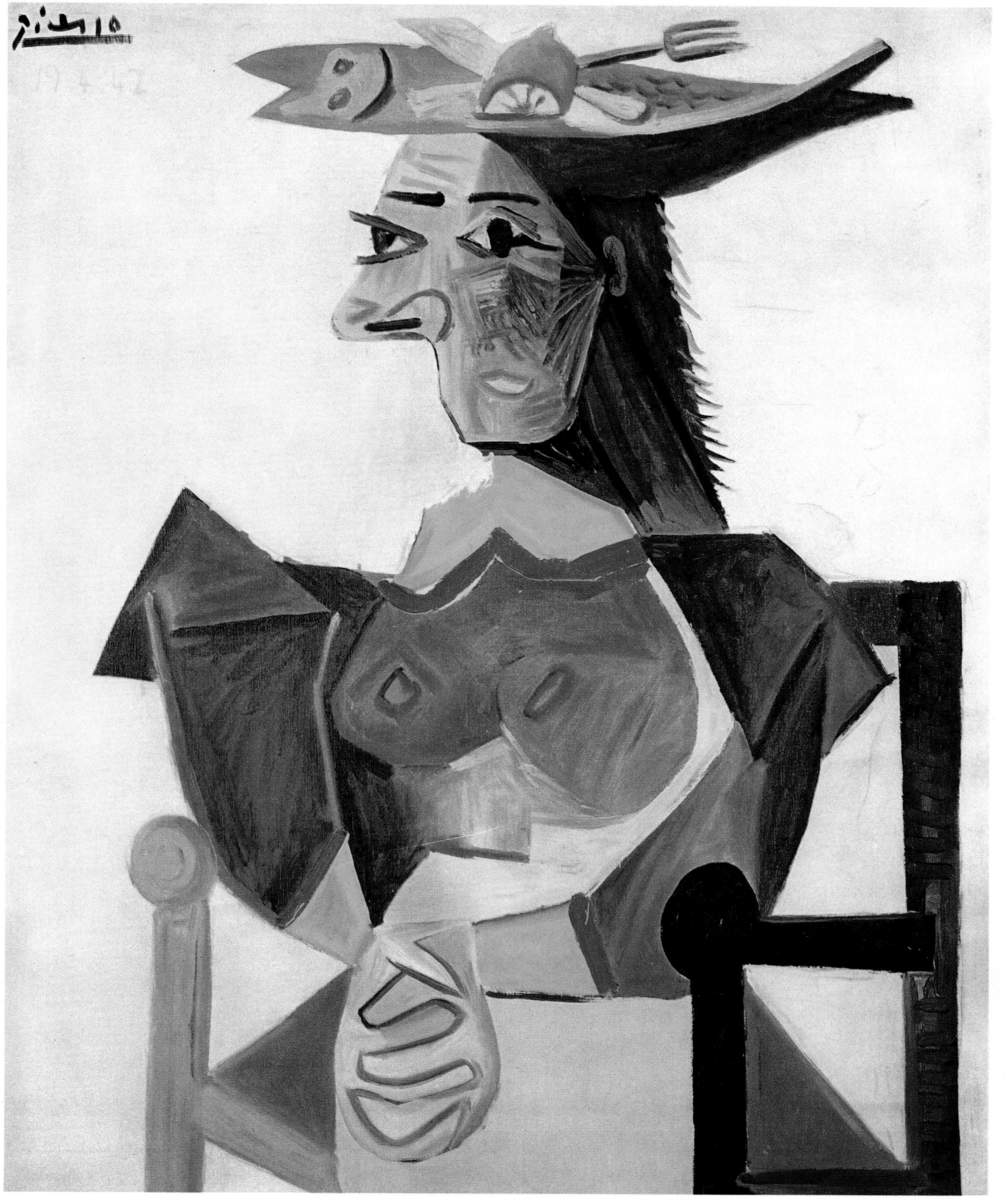

Painted 1945

STILL LIFE WITH PITCHER, CANDLE, AND ENAMEL POT

Oil on canvas, 32¹/₄ × 41³/₄″

Musée National d'Art Moderne, Centre National d'Art et de Culture Georges Pompidou, Paris

On August 25, 1944, the Free French Forces and the Allies entered Paris in triumph. To Picasso, as to many others, this day marked the end of a nightmare: the continual fear, the constant worry over the fate of countless friends, were gone. Typical of Picasso's concentration on his work and of the way his imagination invented pictorial forms for his experiences, is the painting he executed during the first feverish days of the liberation of Paris: a free copy of Poussin's *Bacchanal,* a work in which he found the spirit of those thrilling days (figures 39, 40).

In the fall of 1944 the French artists paid Picasso the tribute to which he was entitled for his irreproachable behavior during the years of oppression—unlike some French artists, Picasso never made any compromises with the occupying power. At the Salon d'Automne of 1944, held less than two months after the liberation of Paris, he was the guest of honor: seventy-four paintings and five sculptures were exhibited in a large room, to honor the master who had been hated by the Nazis and even more by the reactionary elements of the Vichy regime, but who had kept unswervingly to his course.

In those days he took a step that seemed to have nothing in common with his artistic interests: he joined the French Communist Party. In an interview published in *Lettres Françaises* for March 24, 1945, Picasso himself defined the artistic significance of his step: "What do you suppose an artist is? If a painter, an imbecile who has nothing but eyes, nothing but ears if he is a musician, a lyre at every level of his heart if he is a poet, nothing but muscles if he is a boxer? Quite the contrary, he is a political being, constantly aware of what is going on in the world, whether it be harrowing, bitter, or sweet, and he cannot help being shaped by it. How would it be possible not to take an interest in other people, to withdraw in some ivory tower so as not to share existence with them? No, painting is not interior decoration. It is an instrument of war for offense and defense against the enemy."

From this time dates the powerful still life shown here, and the series of views of Paris. The paintings were executed in a vigorous, simple formal language; Picasso has rediscovered things in their modest form and dignity. But he also discovers new aspects of them, endows them with new significance. Thus the juxtaposition of three simple objects on a table—a pitcher, a candle, and a pot —becomes a monument to the quiet dignity of everyday things, a monument also to the creative power of the artist who endowed them with such striking form and the capacity for enduring existence.

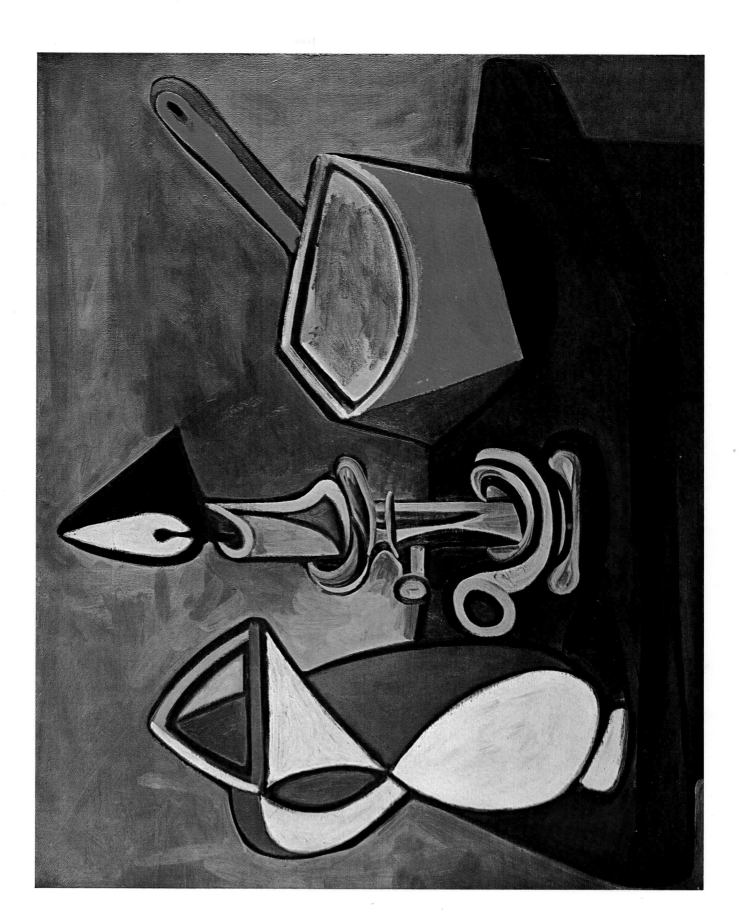

Painted 1954

PORTRAIT OF J.R. WITH ROSES

Oil on canvas, 39³/₈ × 31⁷/₈"

Collection Jacqueline Picasso, Mougins

In 1953 Picasso went through a number of personal difficulties and disappointments. He had to separate from Françoise Gilot, his companion for many years
and the mother of his two youngest children. He lost some of his closest friends—
Henri Matisse, Picasso's opposite pole in early twentieth-century art, and
Maurice Raynal, his biographer and a very old friend, both died that year.

During this troubled time he produced a sequence of drawings and lithographs which, often with bitter humor, treats the theme of the painter and his
model. The confrontation between the figures is continually varied, and often
the humor borders on caricature, but in these works woman is invariably at the
center of the artist's pictorial and psychological interest.

In addition to these drawings and lithographs, which are playful only in
appearance and often tragic in underlying mood, in the spring of 1954 Picasso
produced a sequence of portraits of a young woman, Sylvette D. Here, too, a
type of feminine beauty is a theme for Picasso's constant variations over a series
of twelve paintings. Because of the rapidity of his technique Picasso in these
same years was led to make cycles of pictures on a given theme. Unable to ex-
haust his imagination and his theme in a single painting, he would do a whole
series of paintings, each showing a different aspect of his theme. Picasso's
"series" have been likened to Claude Monet's landscape series and his
successive treatments of Rouen Cathedral—but the comparison is somewhat
biased, for Monet painted these variations for a primarily optical purpose, to
show the same object in different lights. In Picasso's paintings, the artist's attitude toward the object constantly changes the essential character of one work
from the other. This is why the range of his series is so great: looking at the
various pictures, even the non-artist is able to experience the creative process
by which Picasso saw his model in ever-changing ways, and thus "defined" it
in different versions of the same portrait.

Picasso's new interest reached a climactic point in two portraits, both dated
1954, of a young woman whose clear beauty and classical bearing was from then
on to hold Picasso spellbound to an ever greater extent. This was Jacqueline
Roque (who became Picasso's wife on March 2, 1961). In one of the portraits she
is shown sitting on the floor, her hands on her knees; the work reproduced here,
which was painted one day earlier, shows her classical profile clearly outlined
against a simple blue background, on which fragrant roses are suggested in light
colors. In this work Picasso's art of the portrait achieves a special peak, for the
conquests of the earlier portraits are supplemented here by classical mastery in
technique, and a warm human tenderness.

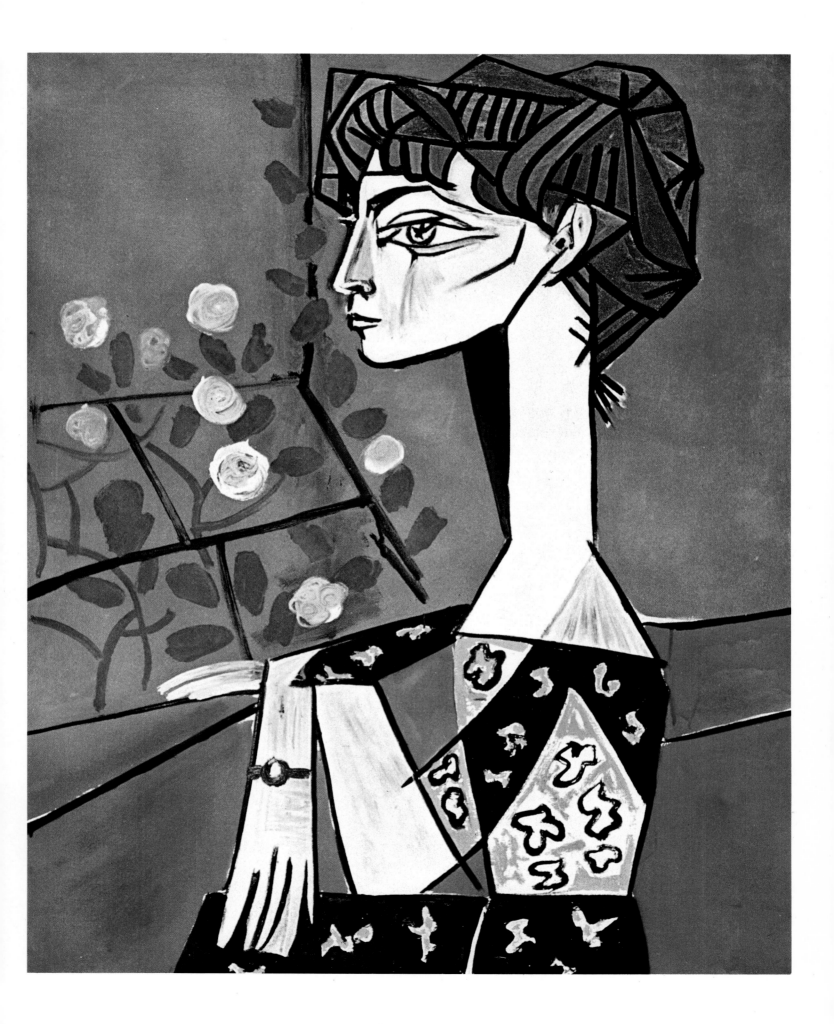

Painted 1955

WOMEN OF ALGIERS (after Delacroix)

Oil on canvas, 44⁷/₈ × 57¹/₂″

Collection Mr. and Mrs. Victor W. Ganz, New York

Picasso's new procedure, which is best designated by the term "variations," led, in 1955, to a cycle of at least fifteen paintings based on Delacroix' *Femmes d'Alger*. Picasso had produced variations on old masters before, but he had hitherto painted only one version of these works, for instance, his *Portrait of a Painter* after El Greco, and his copy of Courbet's *Girls on the Banks of the Seine*. The idea of these variations goes back to Delacroix, and perhaps to an even greater extent to Vincent van Gogh, who wrote his brother Theo as follows:

> *I am going to try to tell you what I am seeking in it and why it seems good to me to copy them. We painters are always asked to compose ourselves and be nothing but composers.*
> *So be it—but it isn't like that in music—and if some person or other plays Beethoven, he adds his personal interpretation—in music and more especially in singing the interpretation of a composer is something, and it is not a hard and fast rule that only the composer should play his own composition. . . .*
> *I let the black and white by Delacroix or Millet or something made after their work pose for me as a subject.*
> *And then I improvise color on it, not, you understand, altogether myself, but searching for memories of their pictures—but the memory, "the vague consonance of colors which are at least right in feeling"—that is my own interpretation.*
> *Many people do not copy, many others do. I started on it accidentally, and I find that it teaches me things, and above all it sometimes gives me consolation. And then my brush goes between my fingers as a bow would on the violin, and absolutely for my own pleasure.**

It was in this spirit that Picasso copied the Delacroix work. However, he did not content himself with a single version, but rendered his recollection of the work, his personal "interpretation," in a number of variations. The cycle thus created shows Picasso's extraordinary versatility, whether he is treating a natural object or a work of art. As the work proceeded, Picasso became more and more interested in the abstract construction of the painting—its skeleton, as it were—and he sought to make out this inner structure beneath the surface. But in the last version—the one shown here—he combines the bone structure and the skin of Delacroix' masterpiece so that they form a single work: the seated figure at the left and the sensually reclining figure at the right comple-ment each other like two sides of the same coin, endowing the painting with full, deep resonance strengthened by the sumptuous colors.

It would be erroneous to look upon this last version as the "definitive" one. Picasso has given us his interpretation of Delacroix' work in fifteen paintings which are interrelated, and what characterizes Picasso's manner of seeing and creating is his many-sidedness, his rejection of a definitive solution. This cyclic mode of work now takes on more and more importance in his art: he comes to grips with his themes, but he never exhausts them.

* *The Complete Letters of Vincent van Gogh* (Greenwich, Conn., 1958), vol. III, p. 216, letter 607.

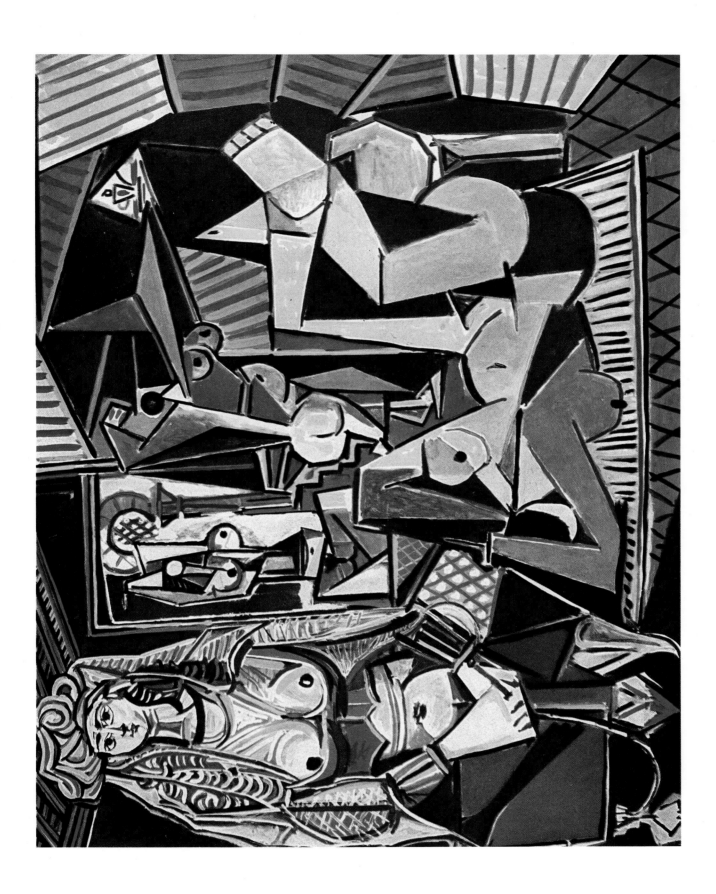

Painted 1957

LAS MENINAS (THE MAIDS OF HONOR)
(after Velázquez)

Oil on canvas, 63³/₈ × 50³/₄"
Museo Picasso, Barcelona

In 1954 Picasso moved to the villa La Californie at Cannes. There he created his second cycle of paintings after an old master (the first being the series after. Delacroix' *Women of Algiers*)—the variations on Velázquez' *The Maids of Honor*.

As a fourteen-year-old boy Picasso had admired this work by his great fellow countryman of the seventeenth century. He admired it again during his visit to Spain in 1934, and the painting must have become even dearer to him when the Spanish Republican government named him director of The Prado after the outbreak of the Civil War.

In addition to the painting's Spanish character, Picasso may have been particularly fascinated by the fact that it treats—in a brilliant, mysterious way—a problem that had often preoccupied him: the painter and his model. Velázquez presents the theme in a very peculiar form: the painter portrays himself painting the Spanish royal couple—appearing in a mirror on the back wall—while the Infanta and her maids of honor come up to the artist to look at his portrait of the royal pair. Reality and sham-reality are interlocked in Velázquez' masterpiece—and this must have held a very special attraction for Picasso.

He devoted to this work a cycle of about twenty variations, repeating this play with reality in his own free, personal way. As is the case with *Women of Algiers,* Picasso displayed equal freedom of treatment whether he dealt with natural objects or works of art. In the catalogue to the first exhibition of *The Maids of Honor,* Michel Leiris observed that Picasso "makes himself at home" in Velázquez' painting, that he himself moves into the royal palace and fills it with his own furniture. But this is not all: Picasso must have felt at home in this painting, for in his *Maids of Honor* there are only paintings by Picasso. Linked to the painting by an elective affinity, he enriched it by his interpretation, and translated Velázquez' pictorial idea into the language of our own century. Picasso not only renewed himself, but also renewed time and again the entire artistic heritage of modern man.

At the same time as his cycle of *The Maids of Honor,* Picasso produced another cycle—the series of views from his window with a swarm of pigeons. The paintings after Velázquez may owe some of their own radiantly bright color to these views. Nature and art once again grow together to form a unity, a fuller reality.

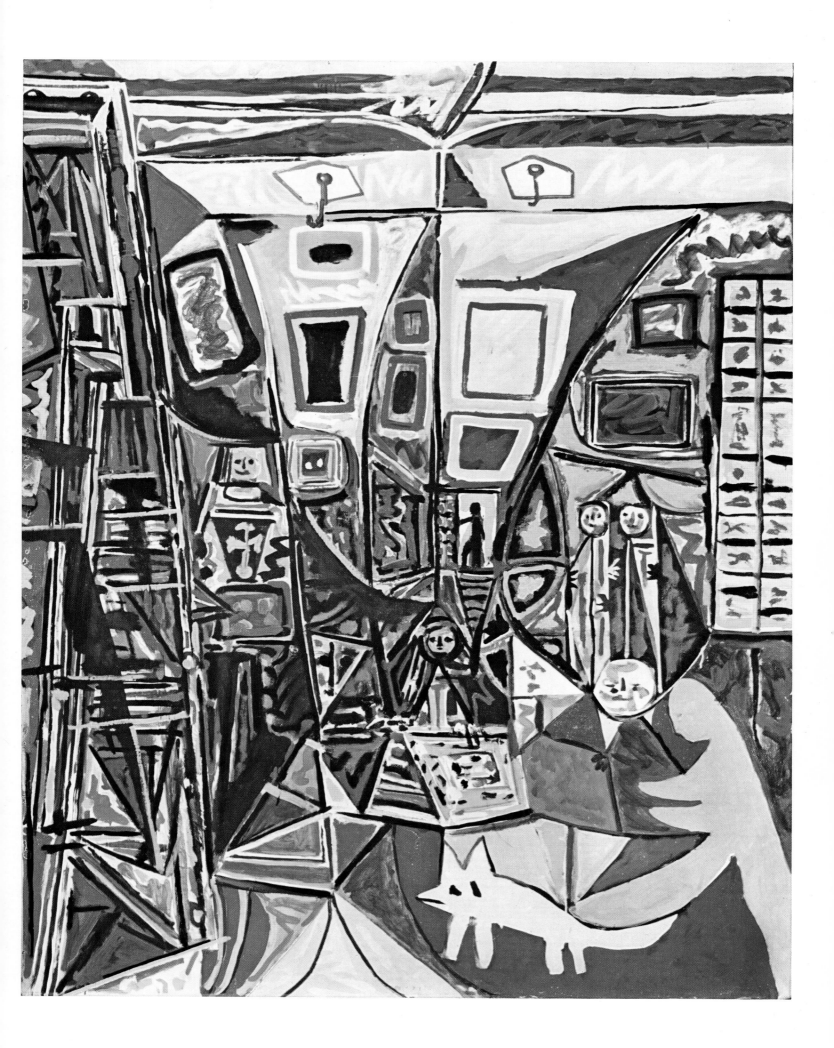

Painted 1959

STILL LIFE

Oil on canvas, 35¹/₈ × 45³/₄"
Galerie Louise Leiris, Paris

After the series *The Maids of Honor* Picasso executed a monumental work that presented him with entirely new problems—the mural for the new UNESCO building in Paris. This painting is a continuation of the mythological themes which he treated after the Second World War, primarily in his large paintings. What is new in this mural is above all the technical execution. It was impossible to paint it on the spot where it was to be placed. Therefore Picasso resolved to paint the gigantic work in his studio at Vallauris, on a number of panels which were to be joined later in the building itself. He brilliantly solved this extremely difficult problem; the mural is set in the wall in such a way that the motion of the viewer approaching the painting brings him into the composition as an active and dramatic element.

After completing this work, Picasso found a new studio. He had become tired of the noise and bustle of Cannes where he had worked in his villa La Californie, and was searching for greater peace and quiet in order to concentrate on his work. These he found in the Château de Vauvenargues, situated on the slopes of Mont Sainte-Victoire near Aix-en-Provence; he purchased it in 1958, and soon set it up as his studio. He moved his paintings and sculptures there, and these contribute to the atmosphere of timelessness which was evoked by the simultaneous presence of Picasso's works from over the years, and prevailed in all the master's studios.

At Vauvenargues, however, he also created a new type of painting, of which this still life is a good example. Simple forms and harmonious colors characterize these paintings; in the contrast between the bulging wicker-encased bottle and the slender forms of the other bottle, Picasso finds the tension on which this painting is based. The simple background of exactly balanced yellow, red, and green areas raises the contrast between the two forms to monumental proportions.

In his biography of Picasso, Penrose refers to the paintings executed at Vauvenargues as those of his "Spanish" period. The fact is that in these years Picasso's ties with his homeland grew closer: many visitors from Spain told him how popular his art was in his native land, where he had not set foot since the 1930s. Thanks to these visitors, the Spanish side of Picasso's character was reawakened. He published three poems in Spanish, and his painting was once again characterized by austerity—a quality inspired both by the situation in his homeland and by the austerity of the Vauvenargues landscape. The *Still Life* of 1959, with its simple harmony and noble restraint in form and color, added a new Spanish accent to Picasso's work.

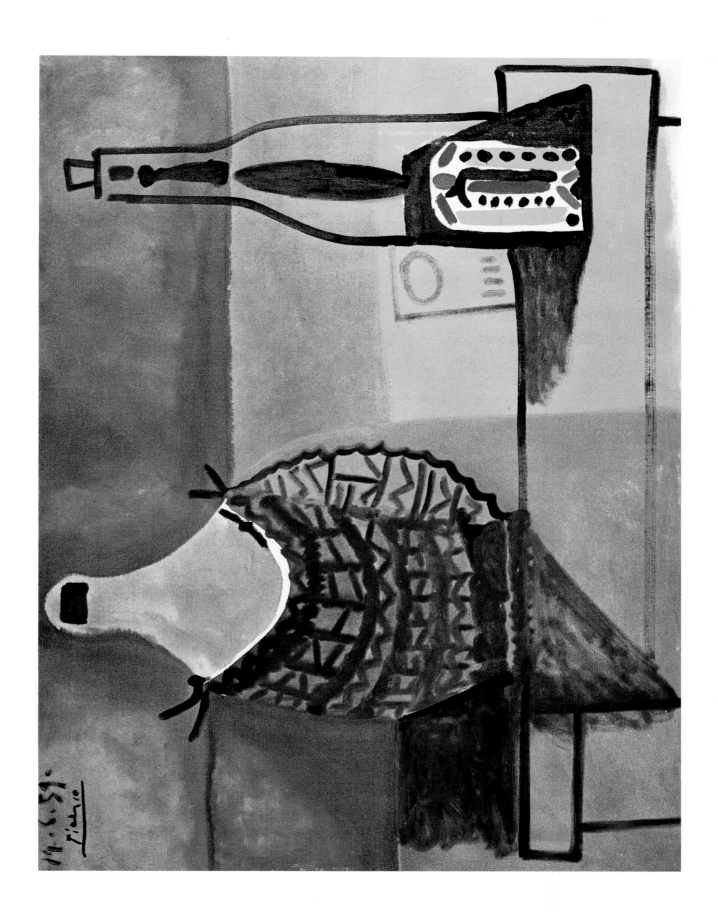

Painted 1961

LE DEJEUNER SUR L'HERBE
(LUNCHEON ON THE GRASS)
(after Manet)

Oil on canvas, 44¹/₂ × 57¹/₈″

Collection the Artist's Estate

This series of variations on Manet's famous work adds new riches to those we find in Picasso's two earlier cycles (after Delacroix and Velázquez). For more than two years, from August, 1959, to September, 1961, he worked on this cycle, which consists of twenty-seven paintings and many drawings. Once again he found an opportunity to take up a number of his favorite themes.

Manet's composition, showing two nudes with two clothed men in a landscape, is itself a kind of variation. Almost exactly 100 years before Picasso treated this theme, Manet, building on a theme taken from an engraving by Marcantonio Raimondi, attempted to translate Giorgione's *Concert champêtre* (in The Louvre) into a contemporary idiom. The Arcadian figures in the work of the great Venetian painter were transformed by Manet into Parisians of his own day, and Arcadia itself took on a new, contemporary form just outside the gates of Paris.

Picasso's variations are of an entirely different kind: he takes Manet's composition as a sort of springboard for his own imagination, which carries him into new, as yet unsuspected directions.

In the course of this work we find Picasso often straying far from his starting point, then coming back to it again, and inventing ever new variations on the theme. To Picasso, Manet's painting—like anything in art or nature—is a theme.

In the painting reproduced here (it is the last of one series of variations) Picasso retransforms the model into an Arcadian scene: instead of juxtaposing nude and clothed figures, we have here an idyl with four nude figures, shown near a pond in the subdued green light of the foliage. This brings to mind the themes of the Bather, and Figures on the Beach, which turn up so often in Picasso's works. But, via Manet, a new background has been added to these themes—the dimension of mythology—and the link with nineteenth-century painting has deepened the relationship between the figures, endowing them with greater tension and thus bringing them closer to the spirit of our own days.

Picasso repeatedly felt tempted to match himself against the old masters. He was conscious of his equality with them, and this feeling gave him the freedom to make whatever use of the old masterpieces he cared to. These paintings show his magnificent ability to transform things and forms alike into new signs, which disclose a new meaning, and in which the image of our time is recorded for posterity.

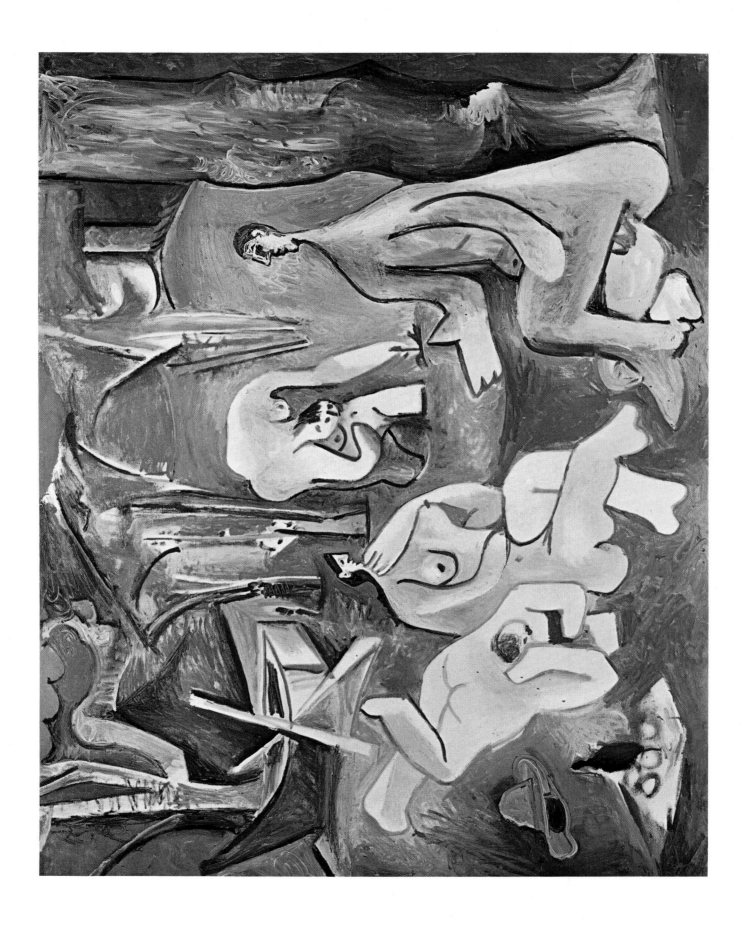

Painted 1972

THE YOUNG PAINTER

Oil on canvas, 36¹/₄ × 28³/₄"

Musée Picasso, Paris

Among other works of the later years of Picasso's life, this painting—completed less than a year before his death—is a model of utter soberness and economy, both in color and in design. The 1964 exhibition of his recent works, and the large retrospective exhibitions in honor of his eighty-fifth birthday (in both the Grand Palais and the Petit Palais in Paris), revealed a trend the artist had developed following his series after Manet's *Déjeuner sur l'herbe*: a style, curvacious and almost Baroque, which can be seen in his paintings from 1962 onward, and in the sculptural figures he made of cut-outs and painted canvas.

The themes of his late work embody three different kinds of subject matter: there is a mythological series, centered around the Rape of the Sabines (from 1962); there are portraits of his wife, Jacqueline, showing her sitting in repose, often with a large dog; and there is the series (done mainly in 1963) of *The Painter and His Model*. After these paintings, Picasso created the impressive series of late prints, united in *Suite 347*, where subject matter of a strongly erotic nature prevails—as in a painting, *The Kiss*, done in 1969.

The series of *The Painter and His Model* (although reaching back to an etching done in 1927 for Balzac's *Le Chef-d'oeuvre inconnu*) is surprising, since we know that Picasso rarely painted from the model. But the thrust of these works and of drawings done as late as 1970 (figure 64) extends far beyond the artist's own personal habits and preoccupations: once more they translate his own, autobiographical data into expressions of general validity. They formulate, visually, the problems of artistic creation: the contact between artist and object assumes ever new forms, and the result of creation is always unpredictable. Picasso once wrote: "Painting is stronger than I am—it makes me do what it wants." The works of the artist's last decade show in what sense this was meant, and the painting reproduced here is a telling proof: a retrospective self-portrait that goes beyond its direct implications, and shows the Painter as a figure valid for all ages and cultures. The eyes, the central and most accentuated part of the painting, look out at the world, and the hand with the brush seems to touch the canvas, as it were, from within, in response to the command of the painter's eyes and conscience.

This late painting reaches back to Picasso's self-portraits of 1906 and 1907. It thus concludes and resumes a creative process begun almost seventy years before, dating from the time that Picasso developed his first personal style, through all his later forms of painting—and yet it has broken away again, in conception as well as in execution. Picasso produced some of the greatest works of art of our time precisely because he—the Painter with his rapacious eyes—did not rigidly impose a style on his models (or upon his own image), but allowed his form of artistic expression to change in accordance with events and experience; because he placed the authenticity of vision above the correctness of form and its language.

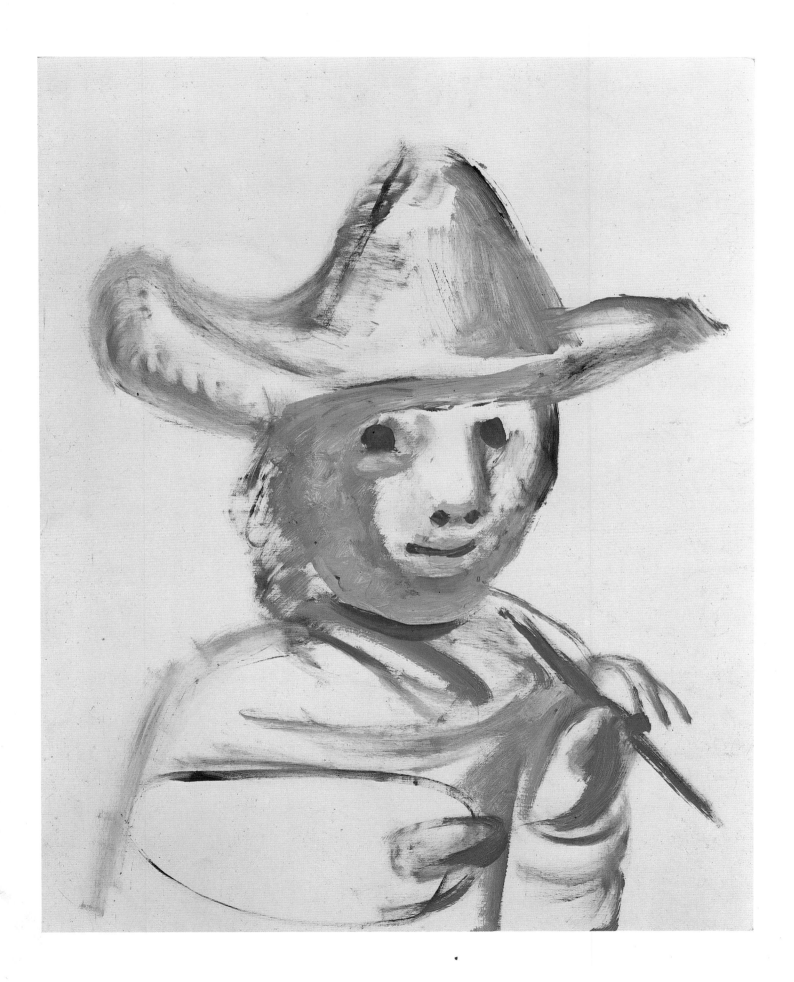